Praise for
H●nest Advent

There is something so enticingly refreshing about the perspective and conversation of Advent through the feminine lens. Scott Erickson's reflection of the Advent season through the connection of the misrepresented women in the Savior story not only is healing and restorative but also brings us back into the story, where the feminine and the divine have always been.

ARIELLE ESTORIA, poet, author, speaker

Scott Erickson does a perfect job of removing the current taste of stale commercialization and male centeredness from Advent. He then brings back in the beauty, mystery, and wonder that this season is meant to inspire. If you want an Advent made for our moment of social and racial awakening, and one that doesn't oversimplify, this is it!

PROPAGANDA AND DR. ALMA ZARAGOZA-PETTY, *The Red Couch Podcast*

When I was an evangelical, I thought Christmas took too much emphasis away from Easter. When I was an atheist, I thought Christmas reinforced an absurd fairy tale. Me and Christmas, well, it's complicated. That's why I love *Honest Advent*. In this meditation on the vulnerability of God through the strange mystery of Christ's incarnation, Scott invites us not to master that mystery, but to experience it.

MIKE McHARGUE, author of *You're a Miracle (and a Pain in the Ass)* and host of *Ask Science Mike* podcast

Beautiful. Evocative. A wake-up call to the mystery of life.

JOHN MARK COMER, author of *The Ruthless Elimination of Hurry*

I'm no Scrooge, but the last thing I want to read is another book on the Christmas story. Luckily, that's not what this book is about. Scott Erickson's beautifully crafted book helped me see God-with-Us with fresh eyes. *Honest Advent* is no shallow seasonal gift book; it's an invitation to explore the divine flourishes of everyday human vulnerabilities. A transformative read, regardless of the time of year.

JONATHAN MERRITT, author of *Learning to Speak God from Scratch* and contributing writer to *The Atlantic*

Through striking visuals and conversational prose, Scott Erickson has created a doorway between the foreign and the familiar, the simple and the complex, holiday and the everyday. On any day of the year, but especially through the time of Advent, land on any page in this book to find a prayer, a bridge, an invitation into what is coming and out of the boxes we put around God.

HILLARY McBRIDE, PhD, RCC, therapist, researcher, and author

Scott Erickson's iconographic works serve as portals to the "kingdom of heaven within us." In this collection of art and reflection, we're reminded what makes our hearts that heaven—the God who comes nearer than we are to ourselves. I'll be opening these doors with wonder and gratitude. Thanks, Scott, you're such a good doorman!

BRAD JERSAK, author of *IN: Incarnation & Inclusion, Abba & Lamb*

We know of few other voices that so powerfully bring back the luster to tarnished, sacred things. Scott Erickson's Advent meditations will be an evergreen gift for the weary soul, calling out fresh and upending wonder at the incarnation, what it meant then, and how we are to be now.

JAY AND KATHERINE WOLF, authors of *Hope Heals* and *Suffer Strong*

Readers on a quest for information can sometimes find themselves devouring books too quickly without taking time to chew, not fully tasting the words and their meanings. Scott Erickson's drawings force us to slow down and open up to truth in a new way. Advent is a season for slow contemplative reflection, and this book will be a tasty treat to savor and to help us reflect on the greatest wonder of all—God becoming one of us.

PERI AND BRIAN ZAHND, authors of *Every Scene by Heart* and *Postcards from Babylon*

There are so many things I love about Scott Erickson, and this Advent book brings them all together. I sense that he is always doing his own work, learning how to live in the body and mind he's been given, making sense of the world through all of the means—psychology, sociology, art, science, spirituality, and wonder—so that when he turns his lens toward something, anything, out come these well-formed, beautifully connected scenes. This lens, turned toward Mary, Jesus, and incarnation, helps me break through the incredibly solidified narratives of Christmas into something that moves me again and helps me connect with the real earth, the blood, sweat, and tears—this happened here, on this earth, in our way, through human birth.

SARA GROVES, recording artist, advocate

As a follower of Jesus who has spent the majority of my professional life (thirty years) working alongside my Jesus-following, Jewish wife within very dark, hostile Islamic regimes, we have celebrated many Christmas/Hanukkah seasons hidden away with curtains drawn and doors locked, lighting candles and reading the Scriptures. If *Honest Advent* had been available then, I would have handed out the book to the Muslim community and walked through the season with them. What a beautiful, timely work of art!

JAMIE AND DONNA WINSHIP, cofounders, Identity Exchange

With the specific audacity and humility of an artist, Scott Erickson's captivating words and images flip, spin, and reconsider the reality of God-with-Us and the transformative notion of that presence in, with, and through our humanity. He invites us to look afresh and find newness and wonder in the Advent story through the female body—not through its typical maligning but as a way God chose to be with us.

MARLITA HILL, author of *Defying Discord*

Honest Advent unearths the beauty and power of life's deepest truths woven into the ancient Christmas stories. Through his gorgeously provocative illustrations and authentically insightful teachings, Scott Erickson rescues us from the commercialization of Christmas by breathing much-needed new life into Advent's themes and ideas. The most wonderful time of the year now has the most wonderful piece of art to go with it.

COLBY MARTIN, author of *The Shift* and
cohost of *The Kate and Colby Show*

As an often flustered mom in the throes of raising four young kids, I connected so deeply with *Honest Advent* because it reveals the nearness of God through a painful but beautiful mess I am very familiar with—pregnancy, birth, and motherhood. Though 2020 will be remembered for a lot of hardship and trauma, this book helped draw me closer to Immanuel—what a gift!

SUSIE GAMEZ, speaker, writer, and an okay mom

The primary job of an artist is to see. And while a great deal of the excitement around Scott Erickson has had to do with his talent for (and with) imagery, what has made his work vital and unique has always been his vision—a vision for God in the world, for people in the shadow of God, and for people in relationship with one another. This beautiful book is the fullest expression of the kind of vision that makes Scott a gift. Good artists have a knack for clearly and engrossingly letting us in on how they see their world. Great artists change the way we see ours. Scott is becoming a great artist.

JUSTIN MCROBERTS, author of *It Is What You Make of It*

As someone who has been in the work of shedding the layered baggage of my religious past, I've also been looking for opportunities to reclaim what is good and beautiful and true. This book is a reminder of everything good and beautiful and true about Advent. Not necessarily easy or pretty, but good and true—and our world certainly needs more good and true these days. I am grateful for the reclamation that this work will bring to so many people for Advent and beyond.

BRIT BARRON, author of *Worth It*

This beautifully crafted piece of art explores immaculately the invasion of the best that Christmas means: Presence in our Present.

WM. PAUL YOUNG, *The Shack*

Scott Erickson's work is both a blaring anthem and a gentle whisper. He takes the untouchable and makes it familiar. Scott's modern artistic interpretation of the heard-it-a-million-times Christmas story invites both the skeptic and the Christ-follower into transformative vulnerability. This is a book not just for the holiday season but for everyday awakening to the sacred unknowns we each carry.

JOY PROUTY, photographic artist

In this personal and deeply felt collection, Scott Erickson offers a thoughtful, contemplative exploration of the wonder hidden just beyond the popular portrayal of the Christmas narrative. Through twenty-five images and essays, Erickson illuminates a deep and personal appreciation of the central story in the Christian tradition and approaches it, not as a creed to be accepted or even a question to be answered, but rather as a mystery to be explored and embraced.

NATE STANIFORTH, author of *Here Is Real Magic*

honest
advent

h●nest advent

Awakening
to the Wonder
of God-with-Us
Then, Here,
and Now

25 Readings
for Advent
and Christmas

sc●tt erickson

ZONDERVAN BOOKS

ZONDERVAN BOOKS

Honest Advent
Copyright © 2020 by Scott Erickson

Requests for information should be addressed to:
Zondervan, 3900 Sparks Dr. SE, Grand Rapids, Michigan 49546

Zondervan titles may be purchased in bulk for educational, business, fundraising, or sales promotional use. For information, please email SpecialMarkets@Zondervan.com.

ISBN 978-0-310-36189-3 (audio)

Library of Congress Cataloging-in-Publication Data

Names: Erickson, Scott, (Artist), author.
Title: Honest Advent : awakening to the wonder of God-with-us then, here, and now / Scott Erickson.
Description: Grand Rapids : Zondervan, 2020. | Includes bibliographical references. | Summary: "From celebrated artist-storyteller Scott Erickson: 25 days of thought-provoking images and meditations to rekindle the wonder of Christmas and the coming of God-with-us. For anyone who wrestles with how we can authentically celebrate Christmas when the world around us doesn't make sense, find here fresh eyes to see the familiar story"— Provided by publisher.
Identifiers: LCCN 2020026480 (print) | LCCN 2020026481 (ebook) | ISBN 9780310361879 (trade paperback) | ISBN 9780310361886 (ebook)
Subjects: LCSH: Advent—Meditations. | Christmas—Meditations.
Classification: LCC BV40 .E74 2020 (print) | LCC BV40 (ebook) | DDC 242/.332--dc23
LC record available at https://lccn.loc.gov/2020026480
LC ebook record available at https://lccn.loc.gov/2020026481

All Scripture quotations, unless otherwise indicated, are taken from The Holy Bible, New International Version®, NIV®. Copyright © 1973, 1978, 1984, 2011 by Biblica, Inc.® Used by permission of Zondervan. All rights reserved worldwide. www.Zondervan.com. The "NIV" and "New International Version" are trademarks registered in the United States Patent and Trademark Office by Biblica, Inc.®

Scripture quotations marked ASV are taken from the American Standard Version. Public domain.

Scripture quotations marked ESV are taken from the ESV® Bible (The Holy Bible, English Standard Version®). Copyright © 2001 by Crossway, a publishing ministry of Good News Publishers. Used by permission. All rights reserved.

Scripture quotations marked MSG are taken from THE MESSAGE. Copyright © 1993, 1994, 1995, 1996, 2000, 2001, 2002 by Eugene H. Peterson. Used by permission of NavPress. All rights reserved. Represented by Tyndale House Publishers, Inc.

Scripture quotations marked NASB are taken from the New American Standard Bible®. Copyright © 1960, 1962, 1963, 1968, 1971, 1972, 1973, 1975, 1977, 1995 by The Lockman Foundation. Used by permission. (www.Lockman.org).

Scripture quotations marked NLT are taken from the Holy Bible, New Living Translation. © 1996, 2004, 2015 by Tyndale House Foundation. Used by permission of Tyndale House Publishers, Inc., Carol Stream, Illinois 60188. All rights reserved.

Scripture quotations marked The Voice are taken from The Voice™. © 2012 by Ecclesia Bible Society. Used by permission. All rights reserved.

Any internet addresses (websites, blogs, etc.) and telephone numbers in this book are offered as a resource. They are not intended in any way to be or imply an endorsement by Zondervan, nor does Zondervan vouch for the content of these sites and numbers for the life of this book.

Published in association with Punchline Agency LLC.

Cover design: Scott Erickson
Interior design: Denise Froehlich
Interior illustrations: Scott Erickson

Printed in the United States of America

20 21 22 23 24 /LSC/ 10 9 8 7 6 5 4 3 2 1

To Holly—

from whom I have learned

all kinds of sacred insights

Contents

Forew●rd

Growing up with dyslexia, I always relied on images to understand the world around me. I loved to read, but unfortunately, the words on the page liked to blend with other words. Individual letters would vanish as my eyes approached them. But this is also true—the pictures remained. And this remained true when I looked up from the book and reentered the real world. Imagery was a gift standing in the gaps of what my mind could not process.

So as soon as my son was old enough to sit up, I couldn't resist putting a crayon in his hand and a piece of paper in front of him. As he examined this stick of wax from side to side, wondering if he should eat it or try to write with it, I smiled. It brought me nothing but joy to see a curious little human start his journey of understanding the world. Long before he knew a single word. Long before he had the cognitive ability to understand "the way things work" in the world. Right now, his focus was on being present to what was right in front of him. And to me, that was everything.

As you work your way through *Honest Advent*, you will find beautifully honest imagery and words that bring this moment to life. You will find that Scott creates and writes in a way that provides room. Room to be present with an open heart. Room to go beyond an intellectual understanding of this season. Room to approach each day with curiosity and expectancy.

What does celebration look like, beyond my modern understanding of it? What wisdom did Mary carry while also carrying Jesus that I am only starting to grasp?

What divine mystery awaits on ordinary days, in ordinary places?

Feel what you need to feel through these pages. Hold what you need to hold. View the imagery, stories, and insight as guideposts along the journey. Embrace the tension of what you know and don't know. Trust that all around this seemingly ordinary world the image of grace remains. Stay open to the possibility of what could be, and you will never be the same.

MORGAN HARPER NICHOLS

Introduction

I. Love. Holidays. I'm always up for a celebration! And the crème de la crème for me is Christmas. It is by far my favorite time of year. But a few years ago, as the twinkly lights and evergreens came out, as they always do, I found myself increasingly ambivalent about the whole ordeal.

We had just finished an exhausting and divisive election. We were overwhelmed by the destruction in Syria. We had an unprecedented year of school shootings. Zika. Flint water crisis. Et cetera. And then came Christmas.

Lights! Catchy songs! Sweets! Cheer! Mistletoe (heyo)! If you live in North America, you're familiar with the candy cane–striped juggernaut of seasonal branding that overlays every part of society like a fresh dusting of snow this time of year. Almost every aspect of Western society is decorated with holiday cheer.

But no matter how many potential kisses lay before me under the mistletoe, none of it resonated. I love Christmas. I really do. It *is* my favorite time of the year. But how we celebrate it just seemed meaningless in the face of real life.

My wife, Holly, and I have been married since 2005, and because of this partnership, I've witnessed multiple pregnancies and births up close—the third one (and last!) being very recent. As we started into the Advent season, I found myself moving away from the decades of nostalgia and visual branding that I had always associated with Christmastime, and I began to meditate on this sacred story—a story about pregnancy, family, incarnation, birth, God with us— through what I had witnessed firsthand as a husband, a father, a birthing partner, a human being.

Also, as an artist, I knew I needed some kind of new visual vocabulary to help me along in my jour- ney. It seemed to me the brand of Christmas had traded its honest edge with sanitized characters in a never-ending winter scene. So I began to create an alternative symbol set for this story that differed from what I had seen in contemporary culture. I needed something honest. Something real. Something with some human grit and a little less green and red in it.

If you're not familiar with the terminology, the season of Advent is the period of four Sundays and weeks leading up to the celebration of Christmas Day. *Advent* means "coming" in Latin, and these weeks are meant to prepare our hearts, minds, and souls for the arrival of God-with-Us, Jesus Christ, born to the virgin Mary a couple of millennia ago. You're supposed to feel the wait—the anticipated arrival of something you want so badly—and by feeling the wait deeply, you'll be even more satisfied by the celebration of the arrival on Christmas Day. At least that's the hope.

Let me give you a couple of personal definitions when talking about spirituality and religion. *Spirituality* is making what is invisible visible; *religion* is the rituals, rhythms, and practices we form to connect to that visibility.

> We make up songs, sermons, little performance art pieces, to help us put shape and physical presence to a happening we find ourselves historically distanced from.

> Nativity scenes are a way we visually remind

ourselves of this ancient story in our present-day homes or front lawns.

Lighting the Advent candles is a way we perceive that the Light of the World has come into our midst.

Songs like "O Come, O Come, Emmanuel" and "Hark! The Herald Angels Sing" are catchy theological tunes that give us a chance to sing together corporately, but they also surprisingly become musical vehicles to approach the Divine with the deepest longings of our hearts.

That's what is maybe surprising about all of this to me—we don't celebrate Christmas like a memorial service but like a birthday party. Of course it's Jesus' birthday, as any child in a Christmas pageant play will tell you, but where is Jesus? When you go to a birthday party, you expect the person whose birth you are celebrating to be there, right? First, because you love them and are rejoicing because of their presence in the world, and second, because it justifies all that cake consumption. The deepest longing of our hearts is not just cake, but to rejoice in the presence of Jesus in our midst today. So where is He?

That's what is maybe surprising about all of this to me—we don't celebrate Christmas like a memorial service but like a birthday party.

I've coauthored a couple of books on prayer with my friend Justin McRoberts, who has a delightful way of framing our frustration with prayer by stating that we can often confuse the mechanics of prayer with the essence of prayer. We can get all caught up with our language and body positioning and forget that these are just the invented structures that help us connect to what prayer is really about—abiding in the love of God.

This is true about all our sacred liturgies and services as well—they are just the visible mechanics that help us get to the invisible essence of the love of God. Often we can become too obsessed with the mechanics, substituting them for the essence, which is completely understandable. It's comforting to be able to hold on to something tangible versus the unseen wild goose of the holy mystery. This is how some faith communities become so obsessed with the style of music, certain ceremonial practices, or just anything that has a lot of nostalgia in it.

Nostalgia is the familiar feeling rooted in a patterned experience that gives comfort in the face of present mystery. It's probably the largest influencer of church services today. It's easy to trade nostalgia for essence. Mind you, there's nothing wrong with the familiarity found in nostalgia. Familiarity is a helpful tool. But familiarity kills wonder.

Human beings are narrative-making machines. Our five senses are taking in way more information than we can ever possibly know or imagine, and our brains are synthesizing all of this information into simple narratives—narratives like, "This is a safe road I've driven down before"; "This is my friend David whom I went to college with"; "I'm all alone in the universe." They can have quite a range of meanings, but they're part of our biological makeup for surviving in the world.

Wonder is an interesting phenomenon, because it's that moment when all of our narratives and stories about life disappear in the rapturous experience of actually being *here*. Actually being alive. Being present with the glorious now. Like when you can get really close to some street musicians playing a song. Or when you pet a horse. Or when you see a solar eclipse.

Wonder is most accessible in new situations, because we don't have a narrative about what's happening. Have you ever traveled overseas? You may know the experience of getting off the train in a city you've never visited before, overwhelmed by the beautiful architecture and sights and sounds all around you, and thinking, *This is the most beautiful city I've ever seen!* Then three days later you say, "I'm so bored," as you board the train to go to the next city. What happened? Did the city change? No, you did. You got familiar with everything, and the wonder went away.

What happens when we substitute the mechanics for the essence is that the wonder can go away. I'm not saying we have to start over every time to keep things interesting. It's helpful to find familiar rituals and practices that keep us grounded. But maybe what's happened to our celebration of Christmas is we've gotten so familiar with certain seasonal mechanics that we've begun to lose the wonder of its essence.

Where is Jesus? If you've read the scriptural account, you know that after His death on a cross and His burial, He resurrects out of the grave three days later (Easter!). He appears for a while in some mysterious ways to a handful of people. Then, on a mountaintop with His friends, He gives them a final commission and lifts into the clouds and ascends to heaven. So . . . I guess He's in heaven—and I'm not going to pretend I fully understand what that means. Heaven is the description of the larger spiritual reality where God

and other spiritual beings are, but I don't know how
to point it out on a map. Is it in the sky? Is it behind
Jupiter? Is it in another dimension?

If you ask a child in Sunday school where Jesus is,
they will point to their heart—and that's actually
not a bad place to point. Not that He's put His bed
in your aortic valve, but in some mysterious way the
center of our being has always been the doorway to
connecting with God. Jesus once said to His disciples
that it would be better for us if He left because He
would give us the Spirit that will always connect us
with the Divine Maker of all things.[1] Connection
with the Divine has evolved over time from a burning
bush, a tent, a temple, a first-century Jewish carpenter, and now the mysterious hidden portal within
you. But was it the fireproof leaves of the bush or the
fabric of the tent or the stone of the temple that connected you with God? Or was it just the mechanics
that helped you get to the essence?

Where is Jesus now on His birthday? I honestly want
to know. This was actually the scariest question to
me a few years ago as I was examining the Christmas

....
1   John 16:7.

celebration I grew up with. I was afraid that all I would find was a love for the mechanics but no real experience with the essence of Jesus. I wanted to have an honest Advent. One that actually prepared me for the coming of the Hope of the World—because I, and I believe *we*, need that hope more than ever.

This book is an exploration of finding the God-with-Us coming into our midst now. What I believe is that the essence of the Birthday Boy is hiding out in the mechanics of this life—the one you're living presently. That, yes, we can look to candles, songs, and pageantry to help us connect to the Divine, but we can also look to pregnancy, biology, history, and mystery as sacred meeting places with the incarnational Christ.

Back when I started making these illustrations, I began to share these images and meditations on Instagram and Facebook and had an overwhelming response—specifically from women. It doesn't take much research to see that the majority of our Christmas imagery has been created by men, and I don't think it's too much to project that those men felt that the reality of birth must be sanitized in our cultural celebration of Christmas. I mean, I get it. A birth is a roller-coaster ride of biological wonder that is not for the faint of heart.

But I do think this sanitization has added another
painful layer to the experience that women can have
in Western religion, and we need to address it and
push against it. Female biology has been stigmatized
by mainstream religion for too long as an avenue for
wayward lusts, a means of bloody uncleanliness, or
a subservient incarnation to those who don't have a
uterus. And yet right there in the text is the celebration
of a woman's biology as the means in which the Divine
incepted, grew, and emerged into this world It loves
so much.

If you've ever witnessed a birth, you know that every
birth is a holy experience.

With that said, this is not a book about the extremes
of birthing and illustrations to put the edginess back
into the Christmas story. It's a celebration of divine
participation through the body of a woman, and it has
been with great humility and reverence that I created
imagery depicting the female body in moments of
pregnant journeying. I cannot fully understand what
it's like to be in a body that is growing a baby. I asked
my wife all the time what it felt like to have someone
kicking around in there, but no words can ever fully
translate the embodied experience. All I can offer is

my witness to such wonderful happenings and my artistic interpretations of those experiences.

This book offers twenty-five word-and-image meditations. They do not have to be read through chronologically, but I have put them in an order that works if you take that approach. We are often used to words as a way to connect with ideas, but I think it's important to offer imagery as well. My suggestion is to spend a minute with each image. Let it excavate you. A great question when it comes to art is, "What does this mean?" An even better question is, "What is this pulling out of me?" Art has that glorious excavating quality, so don't miss out.

Let me also note that I play with spiritual language in this book. When we talk about Jesus, we talk about a man, so I naturally refer to him as Him. But with God or the Spirit, I may use a nongendering reference such as It or They. I do this on purpose to pull us into the greater mystery of the Divine that demands us to evaluate how we speak of It and remove us from assumptions of divine gender. It also is to remove any unnecessary barriers that could get in the way of readers who are trying to find themselves in this story that is for everyone. It is not a diminishing choice, but rather an enlarging invitation I offer to you.

My hope is this book awakens the wonder of God-with-Us in you by contemplating how it happened back then, and also here and actually right now. I hope it can be a visual and lyrical companion as we enter into this season of anticipation—waiting for the coming Hope we deeply long for. And may it be the tasty cake at the birthday party that is still happening today, just as it did two thousand years ago.

CHAPTER 1

Annunciation

Gabriel appeared to her and said,
"Greetings, favored woman! The Lord
is with you!"
Confused and disturbed, Mary tried
to think what the angel could mean.

LUKE 1:28–29 NLT

I presume most of us would invite a divine annunciation. To have some otherworldly being deliver a message from the Almighty sounds like everything we've been hoping for.

How often do we anguish over life decisions and direction, and how incredible would it be to receive a definitive answer from the Lord of Lords!

It would be *the story* you would tell over and over again—how you were sitting in the drive-through line for your iced Americano (with cream and two pumps of classic syrup) and suddenly a divine voice spoke clear as day, as if through the very drive-through speaker, and laid out the glorious plan for your life. Or one night you had a fantastically vivid dream, and when you awoke, you knew with certainty what the next steps were. Or how you tumbled out of a wrecked car on the side of the interstate, lifted by the arms of a stranger who appeared out of nowhere, who told you it was time to do that thing you've been afraid of and have been putting off for years. You turned to look at the oncoming fire trucks, and when you turned back to the stranger, he was gone! Oh, it was an angel! Whaaaa? It would be *the thing* that people ask you to tell at every dinner party.

It would be awesome to have this kind of story in your life. But if I'm honest, I'm actually afraid of revelation. All great stories come at a cost, and the cost of revelation is that it's going to ask something of us. In any divine annunciation, you receive revelation as a gift, yet at the same time you receive notice that all that you had planned is ending. It's all over. Everything will change—most of all you.

And maybe that is a welcomed change. Maybe you are reading this thinking, *God, I could use a change*, and maybe you're ready for such a transformation.

But the rub of revelation is that it's a transformation you're not in charge of. We all have areas in which we would love transformation. For example, me—a never-ending daddy tummy, a proclivity to melancholy, an inability to enjoy the last few Star Wars films (sorry, JJ, I tried!).

Maybe for you, it's your relationship with your in-laws, your finances, your dead-end job with its annoying micromanaging boss, or your unceasing anxiety. But it seems that revelation doesn't transform the places you want to transform; it transforms all the things you dreamed and planned for your best-case scenario.

It's not so hard to see that Mary's transformation could look a lot like ours. How your life would be. Whom you'd marry. What your wedding would be like. Your first kid's name. How people would think about you and your family in the community where you live. How your kids' lives would turn out. Your best-laid plans.

Revelation is a hard gift

give up everything else to

a treasure in a field and

have so you can

Revelation is a hard gift to receive. You must give up everything else to receive it—like finding a treasure in a field and selling everything you have so you can get that treasure.

But then again, she who is willing to accept the cost of revelation finds herself in the deepest of stories. Stories that are so mysterious, divine, and human that we still tell them today.

....

May you receive the light of divine annunciation in the flames of your best-laid plans.

to receive. You must

receive it—like finding

selling everything you

get that **treasure.**

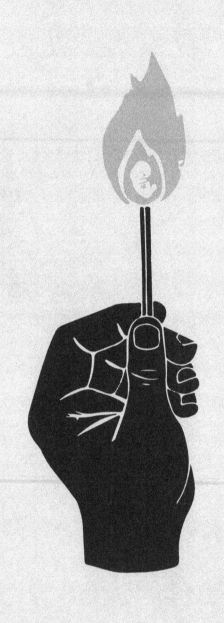

CHAPTER 2

Light

The Word gave life to everything that
was created,
and his life brought light to everyone.
The light shines in the darkness,
and the darkness can never
extinguish it.

JOHN 1:4-5 NLT

The wondrously odd phenomenon of being a parent is witnessing the particular incarnation of each child. Same parents, but every kid comes out differently, and the peculiar paradox of parenting is forming the parts you know and the parts you don't know. You intentionally form in the child manners, responsibilities, social ethics, and good taste in music so they don't grow up to be complete turds in society. But then there is this mysterious aspect of parenting, which is to pay attention to how they have uniquely come into the world and help foster their predisposition to its fullest fruition in greater society.

People come into the world already made. Sure, we are a culmination of body parts—eyes, ears, noses— enabling sights and sounds and smells and all other sensory experience, but there is a deeper, unseen part of us too. We use words like *soul* and *spirit* to describe that untouchable part. It's this essence that's hard to put a finger on, although when you look deep into someone's eyes you can kind of see it.

This is the hidden part of the child you must pay attention to in parenting. And this is the same part in ourselves that we must bring to our Advent meditation.

The Franciscan friar Richard Rohr sums up his spiritual practices like this: "The physical world is the doorway to the spiritual world,"[1] and the spiritual world is much, much larger than this one. His tradition believes there is a much larger reality, a reality hidden from our senses, a reality where God is easily seen and known, and this larger reality is only accessible through this limited physical one.

There is no mountaintop you can take your friends to and say, "Look, here's God," while you point to a giant, floating, cross-legged, golden-bearded man who winks at you and says, "I knew you were coming." That's not the world we live in. There is no visible evidence of God that way here. But if you look through the

....
1   Fr. Richard Rohr, OFM, "The Mystery of Incarnation," Center for Action and Contemplation, January 27, 2017, https://cac.org/the -mystery-of-incarnation-2017-01-27.

Scriptures, you'll find that physical evidence is not the evidence we are offered for faith to rely on.

One of the best examples is when Jesus is teaching His disciples and references the final judgment, where apparently these two realities—the seen and the unseen—become one. He says that some people gave Him food when He was hungry, and drink when He was thirsty—and a few other interactions as well. The people say they never saw Jesus hungry or thirsty. And He replies, "When you gave food to the least of these, you were giving it to me."[2] Kind of mysterious, right? But what Jesus is pointing to is that the action of loving and caring for others in need opens the portal to this larger reality, this heavenly way—a way in which we connect with God. It is through this physical world that we are invited to connect with the hidden reality of God.

I know, I know. We're starting to get really mystical. We could start talking about heaven and earth and which one is our real home. And then I could throw a Meister Eckhart quote at you: "If the soul could have known God without the world, the world would never have

....
2 Matthew 25:40, my paraphrase.

been created,"[3] and then I'll lose some of you because that quote will cook your noodle as you ponder it for the rest of the day. So let's gather back and go here together . . .

Who we are is deeper than where we find ourselves in this moment. And Jesus illuminates that deeper identity.

John writes that the Word (the Christ!) gave life to everything and everyone. And then this Word's life (Jesus) brought light to everyone. Another way to say it is there is a Giver of this life. And then the Giver of this life joins that life, and His life brings light to all life. Don't get lost in all the metaphor! Put simply, the function of light is to help us see more clearly. Jesus' life helps us see our own lives more clearly.

There are many ways this happens, but for one, His being human affirms our being human. It affirms that we are not supposed to be anywhere else but here. Now. In this life. In this world. From being born into it to disappearing from it. This is the life we are asked to live. You are supposed to be here. For another, He affirms

....
3 Quoted in Philip Yancey, *Rumors of Another World* (Grand Rapids: Zondervan, 2003), 44.

Who we are is deeper than where we find ourselves in this moment. And Jesus illuminates that deeper identity.

that we, in some mysterious way, are an amalgamation of something seen and unseen. That we came from somewhere and we are going somewhere, just like He did. And this physical world is the doorway to that somewhere. And God is not only present to us there; God is right alongside us . . . here.

Our invitation to Advent starts here, now—and thank God, because being here now feels really complicated. And hard. And sad at times. With a lot of loss. Right? It hasn't been that long since we all lost a normal way of life. Some of us are still recovering what we lost.

But what gives me hope in this Advent season is the reminder that everything can be taken away *except* that hidden part of me. Whether I lose my savings, my house, my title, or my very livelihood, what is un-takeable is the part of me that Jesus illuminates. The deeper self that was woven into this world but is anchored in a much larger world. In the gift of my life is a doorway to a much larger reality. And Jesus is the Light that shows me the way.

....

May you rest in the peace that the darkness can never extinguish the light that has been given you.

CHAPTER 3

M●therhood

"In pain you will bring forth children."

GENESIS 3:16 NASB

I first encountered *Mary and Eve* by Sister Grace Remington at my friend's house in Atlanta.[1] It was hanging as a decoration in their bathroom, and I was stunned by its message. My friends may have been worried by how long I was in there, but I eventually emerged inquiring, "What is this painting, and who made it?"

It's a painting imagining the meeting of these two matriarchs of faith and what that intimate moment may have been like. It impacted me so much that I did a cover of the work in my style for a Christmas Eve service at my church. So many wonderful theological ideas are displayed in this image. But what I love most is the look that Mary and Eve have for each other.

....

1   Sister Grace Remington, *Mary and Eve*, www.monasterycandy .com/Product_List?c=33; see also "Mary Comforts Eve," Illustrated Prayer, December 5, 2017, https://illustratedprayer.com/2017/12/05 /mary-comforts-eve.

It's like they're at a cosmic party where they don't know each other at first, but when they get introduced, they find out they are deeply connected on so many levels. They also notice they have a billion mutual friends on Facebook.

In this incredible image, Eve is experiencing hope and grace from a brokenness she never thought she'd see an end to. Yet her face could also be that of a knowing mom bestowing wisdom and compassion on a new mom, as if to say, "Parenting is one of the greatest and hardest adventures of a lifetime. You'll love your children and want to have them forever, but you may see one of them die before their time, and it's the absolute worst."

In my opinion, the little that has been written about Eve has been used against her by male chauvinists. In the flannel board story of her life, she gets two paper cutouts—biting an apple and then being cursed as the first mom to go through painful childbirth. That's it. We don't talk about how hard it must have been to do something for the first time. No guides. No mentors. No mommy blogs with tried and true strategies for maintaining sanity. It's easy to knock down the forerunners of human living who made mistakes; it's harder to see through the one-dimensional religious

This divine Gift comes to us through one of us, into the womb of a blessed and humble teenage woman, and honors and dignifies the sacrificial and (w)hol(l)y involved life of being a mom.

narratives that every mom has the unbelievably challenging task of raising children the best she can.

Mary takes the hand of Eve and places it on her belly to let her feel the hidden manifestation of the restoring Hope that is growing in her womb. And yet it's also the movement of sobering solidarity—accepting the entrance into the great cloud of witnesses of broken-hearted moms who've lost their children too early.

I will never fully understand the deep connections and conversations that are shared in the worldwide society of mothers. But this art opens a small window into what that conversation might be like. That *Immanuel* means "God with us" . . . and that this divine Gift comes to us through one of us, into the womb of a blessed and humble teenage woman, and honors and dignifies the sacrificial and (w)hol(l)y involved life of being a mom.

....

Whether you're a mother or not, may you learn from the courage of Eve and Mary, who found themselves in complicated first-time situations. And may you bestow on your very own first-time situations the same grace, kindness, and honor we give to them.

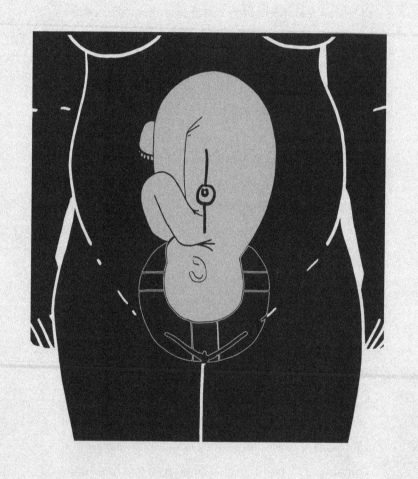

CHAPTER 4

Vulnerability

For you created my inmost being;
   you knit me together in my mother's
   womb.
I praise you because I am fearfully and
   wonderfully made;
   your works are wonderful,
   I know that full well.
My frame was not hidden from you
   when I was made in the secret place,
   when I was woven together in the
      depths of the earth.
Your eyes saw my unformed body.

PSALM 139:13–16

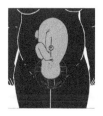

Any real connection involves vulnerability.

Whether in marriage or friendship—or even with a
stranger—a relationship can progress only so far along
the normal platitudes of strength and accomplishment.
It is only when we have exhausted our tales of trophy
winning, when we let down our guards and speak to
the truths about our travels, that we find that where we
really connect as humans is in the places we have found
we walk with a limp.

Even in our work. We all want to attend the conference
and hear the one in our same field of labor who built
a successful and thriving business. But if in the telling of that genesis tale there is no struggle, hardship,
doubt, failing and trying again, then we won't believe it.
Because to attempt to create anything in this world is to
take a risk. All creating is an expression of vulnerability.

Even in our biology. We are a culmination of wondrous

systems, organs, and cellular mysteries that still con-
found us to this day. When all of these parts work
together, it is a delight to behold and a pleasure to exist
in. But when they go awry, it is the fearful nightmares
that prevent hypochondriacs from enjoying a good
night's sleep or the experience of chronic pain that end-
lessly grates within our days.

We are wonderfully and fearfully put together, and it is
only recently through modern science and photography
that we have even been able to witness that process.
The ancient psalmist alludes to an interior process of
knitting—a delicate intertwining of individual strands
over and over again until eventually an elaborate
and beautiful tapestry comes to fruition. We now, as
twenty-first-century human beings, have been able to
bear witness to this in-utero knitting through published
photographs and modeled displays at our local science
museums. But throughout the history of humanity, that
knitting process remained an interior secret.

This interior secret is a vulnerable relationship between
two individuals. The forming child trusts the mother
to provide all it needs—nourishment, rest, energy,
protection—so it can be knit together to its wondrous
completion. The mother offers herself to the forming

child, trusting it will take what it needs to mature into completion while refraining from harming, hurting, depleting her own delicate body of what it needs to survive. Both parties grow together, connected at their vulnerabilities. Both parties take the risk of creating something new together.

If you don't know anyone who has had a miscarriage, just wait. You will. And if you don't know of at least one person who has lost their life trying to bring another life into this world, just wait. You will. The risks are all too painfully real.

What does it say about a God . . .

> who's willing to be this vulnerable with us?
>
> who's willing to come into this world through the statistical risk of childbearing?
>
> who's willing to be attached by a placenta for nourishment and life to Its own creation?
>
> who's willing to wait and grow in the human womb?
>
> who's willing to be fearfully and wonderfully made, just like we are?

Any real connection involves vulnerability because it takes the act of making oneself open to truly be known. God came to us floating in embryonic fluid. Slowly forming and taking shape. Embedded in the uterine wall of a Middle Eastern teenage woman It trusted to care for Its fragile knitting process.

What it says about a God who's willing to be this vulnerable is that God is willing to open Itself up to deeply connect with us. The real question is, are we willing to do the same?

....

May you experience grace embedded in your own hidden vulnerabilities . . . and may you let that symbiotic mystery fuel your Advent wonder.

CHAPTER 5

Given

For to us a child is born,

to us a son is given.

ISAIAH 9:6

John, who wrote some books in the Bible (all best-sellers, makes amazing royalty checks), said that he and his friends saw the glory of the unseen YHWH in Jesus, and it was full of grace and truth.

Truth is perhaps most simply defined as "the actual state of the matter; seeing things for the way they are," and it's fascinating to me that the definition of truth entails having a clear perspective when looking at everything.

This feels really tricky. I've spent my whole life in pursuit of a clear perspective and I'm still working on it. For one, I think perspective often has to do with vantage point. We can place five apples on a table and say that the truth is that there are five apples. But if you are four years old and can only see three apples because you can't see the top of the table, you may conclude that adults are confused about how to correctly count the number of apples on a table.

Second, personal preference always sneaks into perspective as well. The actual state of the matter is that Maroon 5 is an annoying band, but sold-out stadiums worldwide tell me I probably got this one wrong. I know I'm oversimplifying a huge concept, but I think the point is that truth is the end of the journey toward having a clear perspective. Truth is found when we can lay aside our own preferences and vantages and see everything for the way it is. It's interesting that those who spent time with Jesus consistently described Him as being "full of truth." Having a clear perspective. Seeing the *real*.

Which leads us to grace. *Grace* is theologically defined as "the freely given unmerited favor and love of God," which as a definition is beyond fantastic. As a daily tangible experience, I have some questions. Does divine love mean I should expect an invisible hug at some point today? Does divine favor mean that things will mostly go my way? I mean, not so much my way that I become a spiritual Veruca Salt, but maybe enough that my #blessed posts on social media are evidence of God's goodness in my life?

I don't know what your questions are, but abstract religious talk about unconditional love can leave me a little confused about what kind of affections I can expect from an invisible deity. What I've come to understand is that grace is the antidote to the ailment of shame. Shame believes one lacks what it takes to be loved and must endeavor to earn that back. It's the burden of perfection morally, spiritually, humanly, and it inevitably destroys our souls because there is no fulfillment of enough. It's just an endless jog on the janky treadmill of striving. To see Jesus as full of grace means there wasn't any perfection checklist that was met to deserve His presence. His arrival stands against the idea that if you do it right, you get access to His presence. His presence was freely given. He never withheld it. Grace is presence not withheld.

My friend Stephen told me he stopped being a Christian because it stopped making sense. The idea of being created by a God who is wrathful toward you the moment you emerge from the womb—and always will be, unless you say a magic sentence of belief to that God—started to sound like crazy talk to him. He knew he had his faults and bad habits, but if the starting place to a relationship with his Creator was not being loved because he wasn't created perfect enough by that Creator, he couldn't do it. Everything was already stacked against him.

My experience is that many people lose their faith because of their fundamental belief that who they really are—the real—is rejected by the Giver who gave them their lives. It's easy to come to this conclusion, because this is our learned experience through relational failures throughout our lives. Through the failures and shortcomings of our *real*—like anger, lying, grumpiness, and unkindness—we experience the loss of presence in human connection, like someone not calling you back, walking out of the room, ghosting in your social spheres. It's easy to infer these conclusions in our relationship with an invisible deity. This shame we experience can be easily woven into our religion—the rhythms, rituals, and practices that become, not a remembrance that we are loved, but the very accomplishable works to earn back that love. A religion based on trying to earn love inevitably fails, because works can never truly heal the fear of being left alone because of your real. At some point, you just want to be loved for your real—the actual state of the matter of you.

The beginning of the New Testament begins with the gospel writer Matthew's account of Jesus' genealogy, starting with Abraham and running through a lot of other biblical names that are funny to watch people try to pronounce out loud when they read the passage at church. This was written to anchor Jesus' story in the history of the Jewish people. A literary "this is one of our guys" retelling of the story they found themselves in. It's also intentionally showing that Jesus is a descendant of David, tying Him to the prophecies of a coming Messiah from the line of one of Israel's favorite kings. So all the theological things.

I think what's comforting about this genealogy is that it's the antithesis of a polished résumé that is expected to win the job of being the true religion. It seems like it's just a list of names, but if you get into the story of each one, it's a who's who of misfits throughout the Jewish tradition, with some pretty juicy parts involving kinky relationships and murder. It's honest about the family Jesus is birthing into, the *real* human family, and it's refreshingly relatable to us today.

Each one of us, in a way, is a genealogy of all kinds of histories that are worthy of both celebration and regret. We are a culmination of holy moments and juicy moments too (you know what you know), and it is this paradox of interior genealogy that we carry into the season of Advent, wondering if Christ could come into our complicated midst as well.

Grace and truth
is the invitation
to be seen, and
in that seeing to
receive the gift
of presence not
withheld.

The unseen YHWH comes to us full of grace and truth—comes seeing you in all your real, right now, just as you are. Grace and truth is the invitation to be seen, and in that seeing to receive the gift of presence not withheld. It is *this* loving presence given to who we are right now that will truly heal us. It releases us from the janky treadmill of religious striving and invites us to a long walk on the beach as ones who love each other.

This is why the kingdom of heaven is built on the foundation of forgiveness. Forgiveness rights the wrongs. Removes what got in the way. Restores the relationship. Love has always been about forgiveness—*For Given-Ness*—presence not withheld in the midst of seeing the real.

"*For* to us a child is born, to us a son is *given*."[1]

One of the ways we can experience the wonder of God-with-Us today is by participating in the same gift of being given that Jesus did. We too can free others from the janky treadmill of striving by offering them the same grace and truth we have received,

....
1   Isaiah 9:6, emphasis added.

our presence not withheld in the midst of their real. It is this act of embodiment that begins to cement in us the freely given unmerited favor and love of an invisible God.

....

May grace and truth be not only realities you understand but realities you give to others.

CHAPTER 6

Unease

"Let it be to me according to your word."

LUKE 1:38 ESV

There was a moment when the presence of God was felt as the unease of morning sickness. Don't be surprised if your current unease is that exact same avenue of presence.

Nothing can ruin the euphoria of discovering you're pregnant faster than the need to vomit. Although not confined to the beginning of the day, *morning sickness* is the term we use to describe the nausea and vomiting that affects four out of five mothers in their first trimester of pregnancy. Whether it stems from an increase in hormonal activity or a reduction in blood sugar, physicians and scientists are not completely clear on why this happens. The main hypothesis is that it's the body's learned biological strategy to protect the growing child from any unhealthy food and drink the mother may typically consume if she did not feel like blowing chunks publicly.

My wife describes it like a hangover without having enjoyed the party, or the queasy stomach without the screaming adrenaline from the loop-de-loop roller-coaster ride. It's a discomfort that women know is leading them to a new life, and it's bearable because of that deep hope of joy.

It's not written in the gospel texts, but it's plausible to suggest there was a period in Mary's journey when she too went through this same uneasy trimester. I can imagine the moment it hit, ending the spiritual high of angelic announcement and welcoming her into the uneasy, queasy feeling of actually having to go through the physical details of this divine calling. That's the rub of all divine proclamations, isn't it? The announcement that you are going to grow.

The process of growth is always uneasy, because growth never comes through ease. It comes through the stretching and expanding of one's own capacity to push on ahead.

And often the change that needs to happen in order for you to grow may leave you dry heaving on the sidelines. Like when you run until you feel like throwing up as you prepare for the day of the marathon. Or the anxiety nausea of packing up your worldly possessions and moving to a part of the world that is unknown to you. Or the gagging nerves of trying to date again. Or the vomitous

The process of growth is always uneasy, because growth never comes through ease. It comes through the stretching and expanding of one's own capacity to push on ahead.

risk of starting a new career. I have spent years growing into being a public speaker, and I can't tell you how
many speeches I've given that were preceded by a little
throwing up in my mouth before I went onstage. The
uneasiness is not a sign you're doing it wrong. In fact, just
as with pregnancy, it's a sign you're on the right track.

The difficulty in letting God grow you is the trust that
is asked of you when you aren't quite clear what the
outcome looks like. When you intentionally do more sit-
ups or eat less meat lovers pizza, you may have an image
in your mind of what it might look like to feel more
comfortable for swimsuit season. But when you say to
the Giver of your life, "I want my life to be meaningful.
I want to serve You with my life. May it be so according
to what You desire," you have no idea what secret cosmic
strategies have been put into play to answer that request.

You may very well find yourself in an uneasy situation,
just like everyone else in the Bible. Look at the chorus
of human beings in this Christmas story, and you will
see the same song being sung by all of them to trust in
the goodness of God in uneasy situations, just as we
are invited to sing. The only difference is that we see
their whole story played out in the pages of Scripture,
whereas we're right in the middle of our stories being

sung and have no idea if this is a catchy tune or a musical disaster. Because of this, when we find ourselves in an uneasy place in life, our question to God is, "Why are You doing this to me?" Partly this is to check to see if God perhaps has gotten distracted with more pressing global concerns and left us to fend for ourselves. And partly it's to express the disappointing conclusion that our request that God do what It desires in our lives has not brought about the journey of ease we had hoped for.

If you ask a newly pregnant mother, hugging the toilet while racked with morning sickness, why it's worth going through all this hardship, she will wipe away remnants of last night's dinner with a piece of toilet paper and whisper, "For love. It's worth it because I love this child." The answer to our question to God is surprisingly the same. Just like morning sickness, the unease is a strategy of the soul to protect you from doing all the things as usual that could harm this new life being grown in you. It's for love that you have been moved from what is known to what is unknown. It's for love that you have been moved from your comfortable perch so you can be enlarged by a different perspective. It is for love that you have been broken open so a larger capacity of faith, hope, and love can be built inside you. For love. It's because you are loved.

It may be that the divine presence you've been looking for is to be found in your present unease. Instead of missing this invitation by trying to find a resolution to your unease prematurely, center yourself with these three questions:

1. What is the conversation I can have only by being in this situation?

2. What parts of my life have I been able to uncover only by finding myself here?

3. What unexpected place might God want to meet me in during this uneasy time I'm experiencing?

It's in asking these questions that we offer a perspective of divine growth to our uneasy situation and begin to pull back the curtain a little on the secret strategy to grow us into the person we asked God to make us be.

....

May the unease of your stretching and expanding be the promise of divine love growing in you a new life of unforeseen possibility.

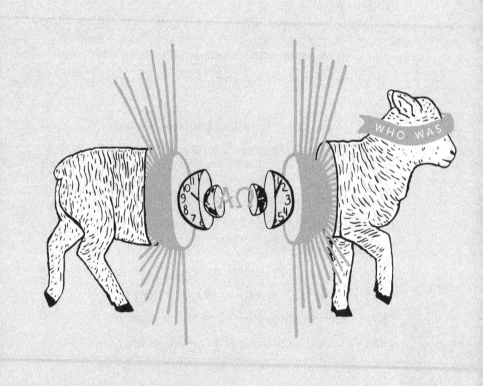

CHAPTER 7

Alpha

"I am the Alpha and the Omega—
the beginning and the end," says the
Lord God. "I am the one who is, who
always was, and who is still to come—
the Almighty One."

REVELATION 1:8 NLT

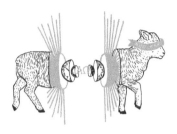

I don't know how God's sovereignty works. I really don't.
I don't know what's free will and what's predetermined,
and how that all plays out. I don't even know if these
are the right ways of categorizing this topic. I just know
that the Divine is really really really really really really
really detailed in Its working with us—and anytime
I'm awakened to this intentionality, I'm filled with
wonder.

This filling of wonder happened to me a few years ago
at a Home Depot. I had been unemployed for months
and was in conversation with a church I had worked
at years earlier about coming back on staff. The conversations with the leadership were very honest and
emotional, since there had been some hurt feelings
on both sides at my earlier departure. It wasn't the
opportunity I had expected, but I was desperate for
some security, since we were on food stamps and my
wife and I were scraping by as I tried to support our
young family.

I received a call weeks after those initial conversations telling me that the leadership of the church had decided to pass on the offer for me to come back on staff, and I was devastated. I hit the lowest moment I've ever had in my life. I did not know what to do next. I had no plans or options. I remember whispering in the dark one night, "God, have You led me to this? I don't know what to do anymore."

Three days later, I was searching for wood screws at Home Depot, and I ran into my friend Cameron, whom I knew from previous creative projects around town. It's only in retrospect that the details of his life make me giggle. Cameron was professionally a carpenter. He had long hair and a beard. Oh, and he was also the leader of a small home church. Sneakily messianic. We chitchatted for a few minutes, and then he asked me how my week had been. I responded honestly, telling him it had been one of the lowest weeks of my life. He paused for a moment and with kind eyes responded that he believed God wanted to share two things with me.

I'll let you know that I'm up for all the freaky weirdness of life, but when religious people claim to be the mouthpiece of the Almighty, I take it with a grain of salt. Not that I don't think it happens; I just think there can be a lot of projections as well. Then Cameron told me something that changed my life. He said that God wanted me to know He saw where I was at and knew it was a completely painful place to be, and God also wanted me to know I had been obedient in doing all the work of repairing past relationships, even though I wasn't going to work there moving forward.

The intimacy of these words broke me. Tears burst forth, and Cameron gave me a hug in the nuts and bolts aisle at Home Depot. Although what he had shared lacked any strategic plan for moving forward, it was exactly what I needed to hear. I thought what I needed to hear was the next steps for provision. What I really needed to hear was that I had been seen and known by Providence the whole time.

There's a section in the Scriptures where John the Baptist—you know, Jesus' cousin who leaped in the womb when in-utero Christ came near—sees his cousin Jesus walking down the street and says, "Look, the Lamb of God, who takes away the sin of the world!"[1]

....
1   John 1:29.

Kind of an odd comment to make about your relative, and I don't think it's alluding to Jesus being rather sheepish at family gatherings. The lamb had been a symbol of sacrificial atonement from the earliest days in the Jewish identity. Abraham tells Isaac on the way up the mountain that God will provide a lamb for the sacrifice.[2] The Israelites are asked to wipe the blood of a lamb on their doorway in Egypt to be passed over by the Spirit of God, which then led to the yearly practice of the Passover lamb.[3] Isaiah prophesies that God's coming Messiah will be like a lamb being brought to slaughter.[4] And then John, explaining later that the One who sent him revealed this truth to him, declares that Jesus is this ultimate offering for God's restoration plan for the world. For John, God's plan had moved from lamb to man, from abstract to physical, from cosmic to personal. And that is the invitation for us this Advent too.

In the book of Revelation, there's a line that reads, "I am the Alpha and the Omega . . . who is, and who was, and who is to come,"[5] which seems to cover

....

2 See Genesis 22:8.
3 See Exodus 12:3–7.
4 See Isaiah 53:7.
5 Revelation 1:8.

pretty much all the things. It's the "who was" part that catches my attention because it means that Who has been around for everything up until now. Who has been paying attention. Who comes into this universe (rays), this time (clock), and this world (earth) as the Lamb who takes away the sins of the world. But Who also comes to us personally, today, as the answer to our deepest question:

Who cares?

If we're honest, isn't that our real question during this Advent season? Not "What was the overarching theological plan of Christmas?" but "Who cares?" Has the Divine been paying attention to what's going on with us, with us here, with us up until now?

Conversations about God's sovereignty always feel removed from the minutiae of our lives because these conversations are always about big overarching narratives involving ancient customs, geographical miracles, cosmic courtroom scenes, and cryptic symbology to be deciphered by "end-times experts" on cable television. They remain safe in big abstract ideas because it's harder to decipher divine sovereignty in the bills, breakdowns, breakups, tumors, layoffs, and food stamps of an

If we're honest, isn't that our real question during this Advent season? Not "What was the overarching theological plan of Christmas?" but "Who cares?"

everyday life. But it's exactly in those details that God's all-powerfulness is to be found. I think wonder is to be found when we move from obsessively figuring out cosmic plans to observing intentionality in the details of where we actually are.

When I was saying goodbye to Cameron, I asked him what he had come to the store to get. "Nothing," he replied. *What?* He said he was driving by this Home Depot and felt the Spirit tell him to go inside and wait. His wife was in the car on her phone, and he had been standing there for fifteen minutes just waiting when I bumped into him. *What!* We walked out together, and I said hi to his wife before we each departed. As I drove home, I gave thanks that God saw the details of my life and had used a friend to encourage me. But it was curious that I hadn't been given a timeline of what to do next. I mused that if God wanted me to be somewhere else, I would be. *Maybe*, I thought, *the real question is, What is the only honest conversation I could have by being in this circumstance?*

That encounter forced me to listen to the deeper conversation I needed to have. As I sat, listened, and prayed through that conversation, I realized that the deepest question I had been ignoring was whether I still thought I was called to be an artist—not just as a person, but as a vocation I committed to—and I realized the answer was yes. That moment in aisle 12 changed the direction of my life. I committed then to the work of an artist, and it is still the work I'm committed to today. It was the conversation that led to my writing the very pages of this book you are reading.

I don't know how sovereignty works, but I do know that God is very, very detailed with our lives. And when we awaken to that intentionality, it will fill us with wonder.

....

May you find the Almighty waiting in the conversation you can have only by being in your current situation.

CHAPTER 8

Breath

"I am the Alpha and the Omega—
the beginning and the end," says the
Lord God. "I am the one who is, who
always was, and who is still to come—
the Almighty One."

REVELATION 1:8 NLT

Breathe in. Breathe out. Breathe in. Breathe out.

Paying attention to our breathing is at the heart of any kind of centering prayer and mindfulness practice. Our minds love to distract us by dancing through future plans or revisiting past memories when we're attempting to quiet ourselves. My mind's favorite move is to remind me of a song I love but have forgotten a line or two of. It's very cunning in its argument to get on Google for a second and look up the lyrics to solve the mystery. This is just the gateway to distraction. It knows that five minutes later, I'll be looking up the weather forecast for my next trip and ordering those sweatpants I convinced myself I needed in order to feel complete. Focusing on the movement of breath in and out of your body anchors you to the present moment and slowly calms down that distracted mind.

The Hebrew language has a word for breath—*ruach*. It's the same word for wind and Spirit. It appears throughout Scripture: as the Spirit hovering over the deep in the beginning, as the breath God breathes into Adam, as the Spirit of counsel and wisdom prophesied in Isaiah, and as the Spirit that came to rest on Jesus in the form of a dove.[1] It's a multifaceted word alluding to the hidden animating Spirit from whom all life emanates. To participate in this world, with the seen and unseen, is to breathe in and out the air that gives life to our bodies, and with that breathing to become aware of the Spirit who gives life to that deep hidden side of us as well.

Throughout the Scriptures, the place to meet the Divine has taken many forms. From a wrestling match, to a bush, to a mountain, to a tent, to a trunk, to a temple—but probably the most expected would be in the very lungs of a baby.

One of the most amazing experiences is holding a sleeping baby on your chest. Sitting, doing nothing other than feeling their little lungs move in and out . . . in and out . . . partaking in the same *ruach* rhythm as you do. We can control our breathing, but mostly it is an involuntary action. It's something that sustains our living while our attention is elsewhere. Same with our heartbeat. It's

....
1 See Genesis 1:2; 2:7; Isaiah 11:2; John 1:32.

happening without our attention. We're not in charge of our heartbeats. We are not in charge of our breathing. So much of living is not up to our willpower.

Imagine being Mary or Joseph . . . holding your newborn baby. Silently together. Listening to His little breaths. Aware of your own breaths. Three sets of inhales and exhales braided quietly together. The sound of a new family.

In.

Out.

In.

Out.

What does it say about a God who is willing to be this present with us? A God who is everywhere at once, a God whom the world cannot contain, yet who has been present with humanity in a box (ark of the covenant), in a body (skull and heart), in a blessing (cup and cross), and in our very breath. "Look, the Lamb of God, who takes away the sin of the world!"[2]

....
2   John 1:29.

Maybe the place we can experience the wonder of this season is in the moments we stop and listen to our very own breathing. To pay attention to the rhythm of *ruach* already inside us . . . and to realize that the Divine with us is not in a building we must journey to, but is in the animating breath of what makes us alive.

....

May you awaken to the inseparable love of God by the very breathing that you are not in charge of.

mega

"I am the Alpha and the Omega—
the beginning and the end," says the
Lord God. "I am the one who is, who
always was, and who is still to come—
the Almighty One."

REVELATION 1:8 NLT

I'm embarrassed to admit it was in my midthirties that I discovered I really didn't care about the planet because of my religious upbringing. Specifically my "end-times education."

If you're not familiar with "end-times education," its curriculum is essentially based in hubris over the details of the timeline of the end of the world. Using ancient scriptural texts out of context, it's a culture of escapism that has enamored religious folk with promises of victory and vindication in a world that feels scary and out of control. It was the bee's knees when I was growing up in the church, and it had a deep effect on me.

In retrospect, I think it's because I've always been a visual learner and I grew up in Protestantism, which is void of any visual vocabulary. But on the subject of the end-times, all the pictures came out! They had charts and timelines and scary illustrations. They even made some low-budget movies in the 1970s that gave me nightmares for years. It was all very convincing.

All this did two things in me: it made me never think of the world two hundred years from now, and it made me never think I was going to have to actually die. Jesus would come back and I would be saved from dying and we would be saved from the responsibility of creating so much garbage, nuclear waste, climate change, and so on. Because God, it turns out, is a big cosmic Janitor! Praise be Its name.

Gratefully, my perspective has been transformed. Thankfully, through study, mentoring, and contemplative prayer, I have come to see these passages not as a proclamation of coming doom but as a revelation of coming redemption. All this to say that I think we all must be aware of the baggage we bring to any future talk. Especially in a spiritual sense. So how are we to understand the Lamb "who is still to come"? How can we find wonder in the unknown and let go of a narrative of certainty that has to do with being on a winning or a losing side?

I think the invitation to wonder has to do with fostering a conversation with the part of Jesus that is yet unknown to us.

We obsess so much about controlling the future narrative because it's a cathartic practice in the face of all the things we have no control over. Look, we have the responsibility and agency to make choices that affect our life now and in the future. I'm not dismissing that important reality. Floss, put on sunscreen, and start saving for retirement are the trinity of yesses you should be making. But none of us are in control of this weekend's weather forecast, the callback from that great first date, our teenage kids' choices, that bald spot or forehead crease that's forming, our job security, and so forth, and none of us are in charge of the inevitable future—yes, I'm talking about the 100 percent death rate for humankind. None of us are in control over this ultimate future or when that transformation will happen to us.

If and when I contemplate this powerlessness, it can be deeply frightening. Besides the great unknowing of what's on the other side, what is frightening is not knowing if the powers greater than me that will carry me to the other side are charitable, merciful, full of grace and love.

"Look," John the Baptist proclaims, "the Lamb of God, who takes away the sin of the world!"

"Who is" . . . fully present with us now.

"Who always was" . . . full of intention to love us.

"Who is still to come" . . . fully restoring us to God by taking away the sins of the world.

Jesus' entrance by way of the human birth canal is the annunciation of this forever restoration. We see His life, death, and resurrection through the Gospels. In Acts, we see the Spirit given to all who believe, and a community of faith (the church) becoming the physical body of Christ in the world, as told throughout the New Testament. We see at the end of Revelation a vision of a new Jerusalem (in art) coming down, and God making Its dwelling among us, removing all that separates us from God, and ruling (crown) with love and justice (shepherd staff and scales). Hallelujah! Gloria! Maranatha! Come soon, Jesus.

But the reality of our lives is we can be present with the Lamb who is, and we can study about the Lamb who always was, but our human lives most likely will end before we witness the Lamb who is still to come. This is the part of Jesus that remains unknown to us. This is the part of Jesus we must start a conversation with.

By bringing the gift of your life to Jesus now, you can grow in conversation with Him about the gift of your life and your eventual death.

How do we start this conversation?

We start by acknowledging our eventual death.

Advent is a season associated with birth . . . but every birth ends with a death. *Advent* means "coming" in Latin, and the paradox of Advent is that while it is a coming appearance, it's also an acknowledgment that there is a coming disappearance. Death is our ultimate loss of control, and we must bring this loss of control to Jesus, just as the Magi brought gifts to Jesus.

Your life is the greatest treasure you can bring. And honestly, you probably don't know where to buy frankincense anyway. By bringing the gift of your life to Jesus now, with hopefully many years of living still ahead of you, you can grow in conversation with Him about the gift of your life and your eventual death. Then Jesus, the "One who is still to come," won't feel like a complete stranger when you become the "you who is still to come" through your eventual disappearance.

....

May your belief in the resurrection of all things trust in the process of the death of all things.

CHAPTER 10

Virgin

"How will this be," Mary asked the angel, "since I am a virgin?"

LUKE 1:34

Virgin birth.

Honestly . . . it feels a bit beyond my pay grade to write about it.

If you were to ask me how it happened, I'd say, "I don't know." I mean, I attended biology class and I am the father of three children, so I can explain the steps two humans take to make a baby. But how that happened between the finite and the Infinite, I don't know. If you were to ask me if I believe it happened, I'd say, "I'm believing so"—because that is the most honest answer I can give in dealing with a mystery.

Throughout our lives, we will encounter paradox—two seemingly contradictory truths existing in the same space and time. Like a catch-22, where someone needs something that can only be had by not needing it. Or the omnipotence paradox, which asks whether an all-powerful Being can create a rock too heavy for Itself to lift. Or the favorite of all college graduates who can't get a job because of their lack of real work experience—"But how are you supposed to get real work experience if you can't get a job?" This is the postgraduate mystery they never tell you about in your university philosophy class.

At the heart of the Christ story is a mystery. The paradox *is* Jesus being fully God and fully human—two seemingly contradictory truths existing in the same space and time. This is the mystery that continues to capture the hearts and minds of millions of pilgrims throughout the world. Yet that mystery was birthed out of another paradoxical mystery—one where the finite and Infinite wove together salvation in the belly of a Middle Eastern young woman.

Why I think that writing about the virgin birth is beyond my pay grade is because this part of the Christmas tradition will remain a mystery and may never be fully explained. And that's okay . . . because the function of a paradox is not to find the solution to seemingly opposing truths, but to be transformed by living in the middle mystery of them.

Your transformation throughout life will be a paradox. One truth is that you have agency to make decisions to change and transform the parts you wish. The choice to do daily sit-ups and refrain from cookies-and-cream milkshakes will create a transformation in your abdominal area. Gratitude and thankfulness are choices you can make to transform your perspective in every situation you find yourself in. You have a choice in transformation.

And yet there are other parts of your transformation that are like a virgin birth—in the way that you're not in charge of any of it. It's less about your mustering up the strength to accomplish something and more about your being open to the transformation that God wants to do in you. It begins quietly and deeply within you. A divine inception in the deepest place where your truest life is birthed.

Surely you have experienced this unanticipated change. Like a nagging knowing that it's time to move on from your comfortable situation. Or a deep desire to try that thing that scares you the most. Or that unexpected longing for prayer. Or the revelatory conclusion that the best way forward is to be kinder to your weaknesses. Or a persistent invitation to forgive someone you feel hurt by.

This is the place where the Divine begins new life. And newness of life is what we all desire. This is the work the Spirit began in Mary, and this is the work the Spirit is wanting to do in the soul womb of all humanity—to bring Christ's participation into fullness within you. To bring *you* into the fullness of the participatory life of Christ.

"For nothing will be impossible with God" was the answer Mary received from the messenger when inquiring about the mystery of how this could happen,[1] and I believe we get the same answer about the mysterious transformation of our own lives. Most of us will not have an angel announce those words to us. But I do think all of us can whisper the statement that the Divine is looking for to do deep transformation and restoration: "Let it be to me according to your word."[2]

. . . .

May all your impossibilities be the very starting point for divine possibility.

. . . .
1 Luke 1:37 ESV.
2 Luke 1:38 ESV.

CHAPTER 11

Assumptions

"But why am I so favored, that the
mother of my Lord should come to me?"

LUKE 1:43

It's assumed that Mary rode on a donkey, but the Bible doesn't say she did.

It's assumed there was an innkeeper, but it doesn't mention one anywhere.

It's assumed there were three Magi, but it doesn't give a number of those who showed up.

It's assumed there was a star overhead when Jesus was born, but it doesn't say that either.

It's assumed that Jesus was born in a stable, but all it says is that He was laid in a manger—and that could've been any number of places.

Christmas comes with many assumptions—some helpful, some not so much. Spirituality also comes with many assumptions, and the ones that fail us are the ones we make about what it's supposed to look like, who is worthy for it to happen to, and what kind of outcome it's supposed to have for us. Assumptions like . . .

> You should be more than you are now to be
> pleasing to God.
>
> Your weaknesses are in the way of God's plan for
> your life.
>
> Your lack of religious fervor is a disqualifier for
> divine participation.
>
> You're probably not doing it right.
>
> Other spiritual people have something you
> don't have.

Our assumptions hinder our spiritual journey in all kinds of ways, and the antidote to assumption is surprise. The surprise of Christ's incarnation is that it happened in Mary's day as it is happening every day in your lack of resources, your overcrowded lodging, your unlit night sky, your humble surroundings.

It's a surprise that life can come through barren places.

It's a surprise that meek nobodies partake in divine plans.

Our assumptions **hinder our spiritual journey in all kinds of ways, and the** antidote **to assumption is** surprise.

It's a surprise that messengers are sent all along the hidden journey of life to let you know you are not alone.

It's a surprise that you will be given everything you need to accomplish what you've been asked to do.

It's a surprise that nothing can separate you from the love of God.

Nothing can separate you from love.

Your assumptions believe there must be something that can . . .

But surprise! Nothing can.

....

May you thank God with joyful surprise at how much you have assumed incorrectly.

CHAPTER 12

Seen

He grew up before him like a tender shoot,
and like a root out of dry ground.
He had no beauty or majesty to attract
us to him,
nothing in his appearance that we
should desire him.

ISAIAH 53:2

Incarnation is the process of becoming seen. To be seen is to allow yourself to be known. To be known is to risk being loved . . . or not.

I remember my friend Taylor saying to me one time, "I don't want God to love me. I just want God to tell me what to do. Because if I let God love me, He will love me the way I am. And if I let God love me the way I am, I will have to see the way I am. And I don't want to see the way I am. So I'd rather God just tell me what to do."

There is a spirituality that operates out of the belief that one flourishes by earning love. That if I do this—but mostly focus on don't doing that!—*then* I'll be loved. Then I'm in the heavenly club, and my club membership is safe and secure—well, until I do that thing I'm not supposed to do. Then I feel guilty, and I need to admit my wrongdoings before the club president and ask for his forgiveness, and then I'm back in the club. But then the next day, I do that thing I'm not supposed to do, and

Incarnation is the process of becoming seen. To be seen is to allow yourself to be known. To be known is to risk being loved . . . or not.

I have to go back to the club president and start all over again. Also, unfortunately, this happens pretty much every day . . . so my membership is constantly in question. It's a very anxious spirituality to have.

Then there's another spirituality based on the notion that it's actually not through earning but through receiving that one flourishes. An embodiment that has dug down deep and found the wellspring of love that never ends and rooted itself in that eternal source. This spirituality is lived out based on the understanding that love is something you can never be taken away from, that love is the animating source of incarnation.

In the image provided, we see a tree emerging from the hands of the Giver of life. The tree symbolizes the incarnation of the Christ, Jesus, from the Source of life into this reality we all find ourselves in. But the tree also symbolizes the journey of growth that every living thing moves through, including us. The symbol of the tree also has a sneaky meaning in that the glory of a tree's incarnation is that it is a tree. It doesn't try to be a hamster or seaweed or a humpback whale. Its glory is seen by all by being its fantastic barky and limby self . . . which is significant! Because one of the qualities that makes human beings so unique out of all other living species is our capacity to reject being ourselves. To hide our identity. To put on a mask and pretend to be something we're not. Just visit any political lobbyist convention, and you'll see what I'm talking about.

In fact, one of the main story arcs of a human life is the revelatory moment when reality strong-arms you into admitting, "Okay, okay, this is who I really am!" and then you embrace that truth with kindness and sympathy. Just visit any AA meeting, and you'll see what I'm talking about.

Why is being seen so hard? It's hard because when you decide to live into your true self—your strengths and weaknesses, your light and shadow, your superpowers and your kryptonites—you are revealing yourself to the world, and you can now be touched. Loved, rejected, embraced, ignored . . . and all of the other complicated interactions that come with human relationships. This is the exciting and terrifying proposal in an everyday life, so that some of us are questioning whether revealing yourself is worth it.

One of the invitations of Advent is the contemplation of God being seen, which is to say, *incarnation*. What does it mean for the Unseen Holy Mystery to be seen?

And because seen, to also be touched, loved, held, known? You might think God in flesh would be the most all-encompassing, attractive Being there ever was with no risk of rejection, but the answer to that assumption is a big biblical *nope!* There was even a prophetic precursor to let everyone know it wasn't going to go down that way, that the Son of God would have no special magnetic look or charm to draw us to Him.[1]

What we see in the chronicles about Jesus' life is that being seen was complicated for Him too. His incarnation was not void of hardship and heartbreak. He was misunderstood by many in His community. His family was skeptical of His new vocation. His cultural spiritual leadership thought He was the spawn of Satan. He even had a friend who sold Him out because he stopped believing the hype. If Jesus' incarnation had been fueled by the belief that love is something that must be earned, these failures at earning love through approval would have been devastating to the spiritual life He was living.

But what we see in Jesus is a spirituality that is grounded in the never-ending spring of love that was the source of everything He did. It was the source that enabled Him to forgive the haters. It was the source that

....
1   See Isaiah 53:2–3.

emboldened Him to meet others in their pain. It was
the source that ignited Him to speak hope in a culture
desperate for a new way. It was the source that empow-
ered Him to lay down His own life for those He loved . . .
which is humanity.

May it be known that the Giver of existence took the same
risk we all have to take daily—to be seen and known as
the person we really are. The risk of incarnation is the risk
of love. And love risks heartbreak, rejection, and being
sold out by your friends, because love is also the animating
source that brings about all the wonderful things in an
incarnation, like companionship, joy, healing, wholeness,
and being seen and known in the world.

A woman at a well once inquired about this wellspring, and
Jesus replied, "I offer water that will become a wellspring
within you that gives life throughout eternity. You will never
be thirsty again."[2] Jesus offered to her what He had received
Himself. He offers that same wellspring to us today.

....

May you never thirst again at the wellspring waiting
inside you.

....
2   John 4:14 The Voice.

CHAPTER 13

Sacred

"My eyes have seen Your salvation,
Which You have prepared in the
presence of all peoples."

LUKE 2:30–31 NASB

I lived in France for a year when I was in my twenties. I lived three blocks from a cathedral, and I'm fairly sure I visited it every day. Granted, it was sometimes for five minutes, but the great thing about cathedrals in Europe is they're always open!

Everything about a cathedral is on purpose. From the high ceilings meant to lift your gaze heavenward, to the cross shape of the building that brings all to the center altar, to the wooden kneeling benches meant for you to feel the mortal bones in your body. It's all constructed to create a physical experience of the story of God-with-Us that has happened, is happening, and will keep happening forevermore. It is built in a way to let you know you're entering something sacred.

What I also love about cathedrals is that they were constructed during a time when most of the population was illiterate, so the majority of the communication devices are pictorial and symbolic. There are some inscriptions and obviously a sacred text somewhere in the building, but mostly it is sculpture, paintings, and stained glass that are the preachers of these sacred stories. And they are amazing! Beautiful! Intricate! Yet they're surprisingly conformist in their style and interpretation of these ancient happenings. Partly it was because of the artistic style at the time. Partly it was the expectation of what sacred art is supposed to look like.

I mean, how *do* you depict something sacred? To make something sacred is to give reverence to the weight of its importance. Something significant happened in our seemingly ordinary world—a meeting between the finite and the Infinite that changes the way we understand the reality we find ourselves in. So to not forget it, we memorialize it. We set it apart. We honor it and maybe add some shiny gold leaf in an attempt to let its message transform us still today. This is a helpful and necessary work that human beings have practiced since the beginning of existence.

My only problem in the process of making something sacred is that we usually cut out all the really human stuff that is equally part of these divine happenings.

Especially in the art depicting the birth of Jesus. Most paintings of the newly born baby Jesus are of Him sitting upright, clean and clear-eyed with a shiny halo around His head. And I get it. This kind of depiction looks way better in a painting than the newly born alien-faced baby the doctor hands to you in the delivery room. And in the art depicting pregnant Mary as well. It's honoring to portray her as well-rested and dressed in her Sunday best rather than just waking up in the morning with an achy back and morning-sickness breath.

We will always take our most important stories and sacredly set them apart so we remember them for

If the incarnation anything, it insists bodies matter

the rest of time. But this process becomes unhelpful when we separate our own fleshy humanity from the humanity found in these sacred stories. Because when we dismiss the aches and pains, the fluids and hair, the naked fleshiness under all the fancy clothing, we can dismiss ourselves from being ones who could also find ourselves in a sacred story. It's the meeting place where the Spirit of God meets every person—our physical bodies.

If the incarnation insists on anything, it insists that our physical bodies matter to God. Jesus was crucified naked. This was an intentional move, since nakedness was shameful, and the Roman soldiers

insists on

that our **physical**

to **God.**

were going after His humiliation. But honestly, none of us want to see the genitalia of the King of Kings when we enter into a communal worship space. So I get it. And I don't think we need to change the art. There is a holy reverence that implores us to put a loincloth on His beaten and pierced body, to return dignity and honor to so precious a form. But to be clear, this is editorializing the story. Even if it is only in our mind's eye, we must hold to a vision of an incarnate God crucified for all to mockingly see or we will miss the deep, deep wonde r of witnessing a God who shared the fullness of our naked vulnerabilities.

Mary is worthy to be revered because she was asked to bear in her body the weight of sacred motherhood, and we will always whisper the wonder of that story. But let's not forget that sacred motherhood unfolded in her physical body with third-trimester heartburn, swollen feet and ankles, insomnia, and fatigue.

Let's give kindness to her body, and kindness to our bodies as well. Because your body, with all its fleshy, sweaty, hairy, nausea-prone, heartburn-prone, cellulitey gloriousness, will be a part of the sacred story you will one day find yourself in.

....

May the embrace of your physical body be remembered
as one of your most sacred acts.

WONDERFUL
COUNSELOR

CHAPTER 14

Counselor

It's obvious, of course, that he didn't go to all this trouble for angels. It was for people like us, children of Abraham. That's why he had to enter into every detail of human life. Then, when he came before God as high priest to get rid of the people's sins, he would have already experienced it all himself—all the pain, all the testing—and would be able to help where help was needed.

HEBREWS 2:16–18 MSG

"For to us a child is born, to us a son is given . . . And he will be called *Wonderful Counselor*."[1]

In 1965, a series of monumental films in the world of psychotherapy was released titled *Three Approaches to Psychotherapy I, II, and III*, later dubbed "The Gloria Films." Directed and produced by noted psychologist and psychotherapist Everett L. Shostrom, the films consist of three therapeutic sessions, with three different therapists meeting with one woman known as Gloria. The films were made to lift the shroud of secrecy that had permeated professional psychotherapy. Textbooks gave loads of information on theories and such, but there was a scarcity of literature on what therapists actually said to clients during sessions. These films let the viewer in on real sessions between a therapist and a client, and they've been a source of education and discussion since their release.

....
1   Isaiah 9:6, emphasis added.

Before his session with Gloria, acclaimed therapist
Carl Rogers laid out his philosophy on creating a particular climate necessary for good therapy to occur. He
said that good counselors must ask themselves a series
of questions before they start:

1. Can I be real in the relationship with the client?

   Real refers to a quality of genuineness that lets
   the client know that the counselor is not hiding
   anything.

2. Will I find myself prizing this person?

   I love the wording here—*prizing*—because the
   invitation is for the counselor to cherish the
   person as they truly are.

3. Will I be able to understand the inner world of
   this individual?

   Can the counselor move around the client's
   world and see life through their eyes? The goal
   of the counselor is to know the client's world of
   feelings and what it's like to be them.

I'm not a therapist. But I go to therapy, and my experience with good therapy is that the counselor has taken

these types of questions to heart. Every good counselor has a heart of empathy for one's situation and how they got there, but also a zeal for the individual to become healed from deep trauma and to walk down the road to a restored, healthy self. At least that's what we pay them for.

These questions remind me of the musings in the book of Hebrews, where the author uses the metaphor of a high priest in his interpretation of Jesus' life. A high priest was one who was selected every year to offer the atoning sacrifices for the entire nation of Israel. He had to take on the mantle of awareness of wrongdoing and be the confessor in hopes of restoration between the people and YHWH. A heavy burden to bear, for sure.

What is interesting in the connections that the author makes between the high priest and Jesus is the qualities of such a go-between.

The author states that the high priest "can deal gently with the ignorant and misguided, since he himself also is beset with weakness."[2] He says Jesus was tempted like we are, so "He is able to come to the aid of those

....
2   Hebrews 5:2 NASB.

who are tempted."[3] The author adds that "we do not have a high priest who is unable to empathize with our weaknesses"[4]—and thank God we don't, because how could we ever experience deep therapy with One who could not understand what it's like to move around in our world and see it through our own eyes? It sounds like the goal of a good therapist and the goal of a successful high priest are the same—to prize the ones who are being healed.

Rogers said that if these attitudes are present in the counselor, quite a number of things will happen in the session:

1. The client will be free to explore their attitudes and feelings more deeply.

2. The client will be able to discover hidden aspects of themselves that they weren't aware of before.

3. Feeling prized by the counselor, the client will come to a deeper prizing of themselves. (I love this one!)

....
3   Hebrews 2:18 NASB.
4   Hebrews 4:15.

4. If the client senses a realness in the counselor, they'll be able to be a little more real within themselves.

5. Feeling that some of their meanings are understood, the client will be more readily available to listen to themselves and their experiences and find some of the meanings they hadn't been able to catch before.

6. From being disapproving of themselves the client will move to a greater acceptance of themselves.

The author of Hebrews summarizes his comparison of Jesus and the good high priest with an invitation: "Let us then approach God's throne of grace with confidence, so that we may receive mercy and find grace to help us in our time of need"[5]—and I can't help but think of this as the perfect description of some of my most healing therapy sessions. A space where I was seen, heard, known, and prized, which then allowed me to enter into a terrain of freedom in which I could experience healing and movement toward wholistic restoration.

Maybe this Advent, we can see the incarnation of Jesus

....
5   Hebrews 4:16.

as the very way He is answering these questions as a Wonderful Counselor. He became human so we would know He had nothing to hide. He lived in a complicated world so He could relate to the complexity of being in our world. His name is God-with-Us so we would know we are prized and in that feeling of being prized would come to a deeper prizing of ourselves.

....

May grace for human weakness allow you to become who you were born to be.

Jesus became **human** so we would know He had nothing to hide. He lived in a complicated world so He could **relate** to the complexity of being in our **world.** His name is **God-with-Us** so we would know we are **prized.**

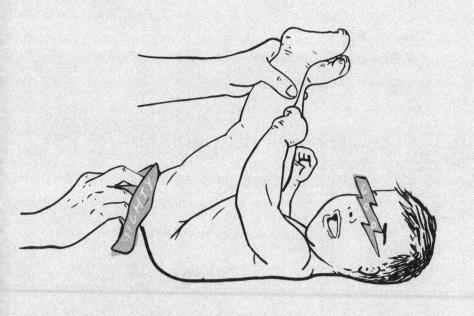

CHAPTER 15

Mighty

In your relationships with one another,
have the same mindset as Christ Jesus:
Who, being in very nature God,
    did not consider equality with God
        something to be used to his
        own advantage;
rather, he made himself nothing
    by taking the very nature of a servant,
    being made in human likeness.
And being found in appearance as a man,
    he humbled himself
    by becoming obedient to death—
        even death on a cross!

PHILIPPIANS 2:5–8

"For to us a child is born, to us a son is given . . . And he will be called . . . *Mighty God*."[1]

If you live long enough, your life will begin and end with someone wiping your butt. From vulnerability to vulnerability we live . . . that is to say, weakness will be a companion throughout our lives. It will take different forms at various stages of development, but the irony is that it may come full circle at the end with bowel management.

Your life starts as a baby in complete vulnerability. Existence is accomplished only with the help of others. But as you get older, you learn that poop goes in the potty, training wheels need to come off in order to go faster, and the world is much, much larger and more complicated than you could ever imagine.

Then puberty hits without your knowing it, and no

....
1   Isaiah 9:6, emphasis added.

one tells you that the vulnerability of this time is the complete displacement from everything you've learned about the world, others, and even yourself. Your young adulthood is spattered with vulnerabilities in love, relationships, finances, career, and the sense of who you want to be in the world, but the good news is that you'll probably look the best you'll ever look in your life.

Your thirties and forties give you a deeper sense of self, but this gift is intertwined with the vulnerabilities of marriages not working out, careers ending abruptly, and life not turning out the way you thought it would. Oh, also, when you turn forty, your knees go into retirement. I'm not beyond my forties, but the vulnerabilities ahead seem to involve the heartbreak of children moving on, the unknown of what happens after retirement, a continued diminishment in physicality, and a growing familiarity with the conversation about your eventual death.

I'm aware that this is a gross summation of a human life, but it's important to hit on at least some of the highlights when we come to the title of Mighty God.

What do we think about when we hear the words *Mighty God*? *Mighty* is another word for strength, and there are plenty of stories of the strength of God in the Bible.

Strength over the elements and armies and powers—it's
not hard to understand how our idea of God can start
to resemble a superhero motif. Less spandex and more
drapery, mind you, but I think when most people imagine
God, they imagine a kind of Superman version of God—
One who is able to conquer the enemies, cast out the evil
spirits, and make more wine for the party in a single blow!

But if Jesus is a vision of the invisible Almighty, what does
His incarnation tell us about a Mighty God? Is *mighty*
referring to His physicality, personality, spirituality?

I know there's the one story where Jesus knocks over some
tables, but you don't see mightiness embodied in physicality very much in His story. In fact, the opposite is often
true—images of One who is a suffering servant, who
is like a lamb being led to slaughter, who is obedient to
death, as Paul writes to the Philippian believers—because
mightiness isn't necessarily something that physically overcomes so much as it is the strength to go through.

Most superhero stories end with powerful heroes fight-
ing, punching, and kicking other powerful foes into
submission to bring about an end to something terrible.
Granted, the terrible forces of comic books are mostly
giant lasers or planet-eating giants, which is not exactly

real life. The motif is built on weight lifters with amazing hair who look awesome in colorful spandex outfits.

But I ran across a comic book once that did not go this way. It's called *Superman: Peace on Earth*, and in it the writer and illustrator Alex Ross shows Superman attempting to solve world hunger, a problem applicable to today. It's a long story, and (spoiler alert!) Superman cannot solve world hunger. The problem is not his strength or his physicality. The problem is not that there isn't enough food or a way to get it to people. The problem is the greed in selfish human hearts. And Superman, even with all his strength, cannot overcome the human heart with his bulging muscles.

If Jesus embodied mightiness through an overcoming through physicality, He would've appeared in a golden onesie, ripped like a CrossFit trainer, kicking the can of anyone in His way. But instead we find a humble servant wrapped in human vulnerability who is obedient to that vulnerability all the way to death, even if it happens to be death on a cross. Jesus is mighty not because of His capacity to overcome hardship but because of His willingness to go through human hardship, like we have to do. It is this compassionate empathy that has the power to transform the human heart.

Jesus is mighty not because of His capacity to overcome hardship but because of His willingness to go through human hardship, like we have to do.

How does God restore what It loves? By being with what God loves.

How does love defeat its enemy, death? By accepting it and going through it.

How does God show Itself to be mighty? God humbles Itself and owns being human. God accepts the humility and weakness of being born. God accepts the humility and vulnerability of eventually dying. And it is this mighty ground that God saves the world through.

Could it be that the doorway to experiencing God-with-Us this Advent is the particular vulnerability we find ourselves facing? Whether it's in health, heart, or home, our lives will always have a particular vulnerability to them—from butt wiping to butt wiping. May we not see this vulnerability as the place of failure because of our inability to overcome it, but as the very invitation to partner with Mighty God through it.

....

May your present stage of life be the mighty ground for divine participation.

CHAPTER 16

Father

In the beginning was the Word,
and the Word was with God, and the
Word was God. He was with God in the
beginning. Through him all things were
made; without him nothing was made
that has been made.

JOHN 1:1–3

"For to us a child is born, to us a son is given . . . And he will be called . . . *Everlasting Father*."[1]

No one really knows what happened to Jesus' dad Joseph. He's around at the beginning when Jesus is a kid, but then he's absent from the story during Jesus' ministry years. He most likely died. There are legends and rumors and such . . . but no one really knows.

It seems like it's only in the telling of the story of Jesus' birth that we get any real picture of Joseph. He cares for Mary, and his plan to separate from her secretly was so he wouldn't disgrace her name. We know he's got some royal blood, being in the Davidic line, and that's what brings them to Jerusalem during the census. He listens to the voice of God and makes life-altering decisions because of this. He's a carpenter, an artisan, and a provider to a family of many kids. He

....
1 Isaiah 9:6, emphasis added.

seems like a great guy. I wonder what Jesus thinks of him . . .

It's a simple fact that everyone has parents. I know not everyone has two parents around, but we are all the by-product of two people—and that comes with a lot of wonder, weirdness, and weight.

It's a wonder that we are our own person, but we can see so much of our parents in ourselves in the way we act and look. Their imprint is unquestionable, whether we like it or not.

It's weird because family is something you don't get any choice in. You just appear in an inherent connection with these other people for the rest of your life. You can have closer relationships with other individuals, but it's only a very small group of people in all the world who will be your family, and an even smaller group you will call your parents. They will eventually die (like everything), but they're always your parents.

Also, if you partake in naked midnight wrestling, you may become a parent yourself, and you'll feel the immense weight of that responsibility. It's scary, wonderful, risky, completely humbling and decentering, and at times entirely engrossing. I've already been interrupted seven times just writing this so far.

But one thing never changes—you *have* parents forever and may *be* a parent forever. You are connected to the two people you are a genetic combination of until the end of time, and if you produce life and become a parent, you will forever be relationally connected to that life you made. You can never stop having parents. And if you have children, you will never stop being a parent.

Jesus Christ died as a single man with no kids. And yet this prophetic word calls Him "Everlasting Father." I don't know if the mystery of this title will come to any full understanding anytime soon, but let us sit with the wonder of His name.

Jesus—the One who is, and who was, and who is to come—is forever relationally a child of parents. He had parents. He has parents. They will forever be His parents.

And . . .

Christ is forever a parent to all of creation. In his first chapter, the gospel writer John proclaims, "All things came into being through Him, and apart from Him nothing came into being that has come into being."[2] Everything is relationally tied to Him. Including us. We can never not be tied to Him.

Therefore the incarnation of Jesus Christ is the answer to our deepest question . . .

Am I an orphan to this existence?

His twofold answer comes in the record of His life lived out in ancient Palestine and in His very cosmic presence now through which all things were made. He can never stop having a father, and He can never stop being a Father. And out of all the titles we could have given Him, apparently "Father" was one of the ones we needed the most.

. . . .

May you live into your true inheritance as the beloved offspring of the Maker of all things.

. . . .
2   John 1: 3 NASB.

P
E

PRI   NCE

A
C
E

CHAPTER 17

Peace

When King Herod heard this he was
disturbed, and all Jerusalem with him.

MATTHEW 2:3

PRI NCE

ACE

"For to us a child is born, to us a son is given, and the government will be on his shoulders. And he will be called . . . *Prince of Peace*. Of the greatness of his government and peace there will be no end."[1]

A government is a system of rule that implements the strategies and policies created to propagate healthy and wholistic ways of living together. Peace in this government can be accomplished a few ways.

You can destroy everyone who has differing opinions about *your way*—eradicating all innate agency and uniqueness found in the world—and end up with a government based on the rule of compliance and the threat of shameful destruction. *A kingdom of fear.*

Or you can love the hell out of everyone by eternally offering your naked vulnerable self as a loving way that

....
1 Isaiah 9:6–7, emphasis added.

134

overcomes fear, selfishness, greed, and death—prizing all innate agency and uniqueness found in the world as the very cornerstones on which to build a government focused on loving one another as one would love themselves. *A kingdom of heaven.*

This second government was illuminated on the shoulders of a naked newborn prince. The announcement scared the powers so much that they killed innocent baby boys in the hope of snuffing out this incarnation. Later on, the powers successfully killed this incarnation in the hope that this way of being in the world would never catch on.

Two thousand years later, the powers are still trying to kill that way of being in the world. Two thousand years later, the kingdom of heaven still lives.

....

May Your kingdom, Jesus, be on earth as it is in heaven.

CHAPTER 18

With

Then the angel showed me a river
with the water of life, clear as crystal,
flowing from the throne of God and of
the Lamb. It flowed down the center
of the main street. On each side of the
river grew a tree of life, bearing twelve
crops of fruit . . . The leaves were used
for medicine to heal the nations.

REVELATION 22:1–2 NLT

I was discussing future schedules with a very pregnant photographer friend of mine, and in the middle of our conversation, she blurted out, "Well, there's a baby coming, and there's nothing I can do about it!"

It was meant as a joke, but it hit me deep, because what she was also saying was, "My life is going to change, no matter what."

In that conversation, what she was alluding to was that a new human was forming, maturing, growing inside of her, and one day it would eventually work its way out and be with the world we all know and live in. On that day, the lives of my friend and her husband would be irrevocably changed. For the better they hoped.

But her statement revealed a truth unfolding right now for all of us: there are many powers, forces, presences that impact our lives daily, and there is nothing we can do to stop that impact.

For example, cosmically . . . the sun will burn out all of its hydrogen approximately five billion years from now, and there is nothing you can do about it. Don't take it personally. It's just the nature of stars.

On a smaller scale, though, the seasons change outside of our control. And toddlers turn into teenagers. And you get uncontrollable giggles at inappropriate times. A song that holds a personal history for you pops on the radio, and suddenly you feel sad. You get blindsided by a distracted driver on a Thursday. You get caught in the rain with all the groceries still in the car. You experience a holy moment. Your hair turns gray. Your parents die. The sun rises. You fall in love.

There is so much we don't have control over, and it will change us no matter what. What we do have is the agency to respond to these forces. The ability to decide how we are going to let them change us—for better or for worse.

A baby named Jesus came, and there is nothing you can do about it, but you do have the agency to respond to that coming, which is partly why I think you are reading this book. Sometimes I think insecurity in religion can make this coming into a needless membership

139

sign-up opportunity. "Baby Jesus came—do you believe it, or do you not?" But I think the deeper question we can contemplate in this season is this: Does God want to change us for the better or for the worse through the gift of this incarnation? Through the gift of God-with-Us? And if for the better, how so?

The answer to how we change for the better is found in the word *with*.

My friends are changed—yes, because of a baby—but they are changed for the better because that child will be with them throughout their lives. They will give to her, and she will give to them. They will nourish her, and she will nourish them. They will grow by her, and she will grow by them. They are irrevocably changed for the better because of her being *with* them.

There's a prophetic word about the coming Messiah in the book of Isaiah that says, "Out of the stump of David's family will grow a shoot—yes, a new Branch bearing fruit from the old root."[1] It's a delight-ful visual—new life emerging from something that had been cut down—and it fits beautifully in the

....
1 Isaiah 11:1 NLT.

overarching metaphor of a tree at the heart of union with God.

Remember, in an ancient context, you received nourishment from trees. There was no grocery store, save for trees, where you could squeeze all of the avocados to find the ripest one. The symbol of the tree is the symbol of sustaining life. The Genesis story has a tree at the center of the garden whose fruit gives life to all who eat of it.[2] Then, in the very last chapter of the vision in Revelation, there is a tree whose fruit is used for the healing of everyone.[3] From the beginning to the very end, the symbol of the tree in our midst is the promise of sustaining life everlasting. That tree is always *with* us.

Change will come, but it is not absent from life-giving connection. How wondrous is it to contemplate in this season that the tree of life was at one time connected to another tree of life? That this symbiotic with-ness gloriously proclaims we will never have to do transformation alone.

....

May you see that you never have to do it alone.

....

2   See Genesis 2:9.
3   See Revelation 22:2.

CHAPTER 19

Room

While they were there, the time came for the baby to be born, and she gave birth to her firstborn, a son. She wrapped him in cloths and placed him in a manger, because there was no guest room available for them.

LUKE 2:6–7

"There was no room for them in the inn" is possibly one of the most excavating reveals of this story and perhaps the most misunderstood.

The misunderstanding comes from years of evolving storytelling and our chronological distance from an ancient Middle Eastern context. Their society did not run like our twenty-first century does. Our traditional telling, fueled mostly by Renaissance paintings and children's Christmas plays at church, would have us believe that pregnant Mary and "no speaking lines" Joseph are hurriedly making their way to Bethlehem because this baby is about to pop. But because of the Roman census, all the Holiday Inn Express hotels and La Quinta inns were booked.

Thankfully, one kind hotel manager had a big enough heart to offer his stable to them (rent-free!) so Mary could give birth to the baby Jesus while a donkey and an ox watched from their hay-filled beds. Oh, and some shepherds showed up later for the inaugural baby visit and brought along their sheep, who also have no speaking lines in the play but look really cute in their cotton-ball costumes.

Although this story line works pleasantly in a thirty-five-minute, small-budget parish production, it's most likely not the way it went down. Mary and Joseph did go to Jerusalem for the census, but they were not in a hurry. The text says, "While they were there, the days were completed,"[1] meaning they were in Bethlehem for a while waiting for the baby to come in His own time.

And they weren't alone. In this ancient society, family stayed with family—especially pregnant ones. We exist in a highly individualized society where it's normal not to stay overnight in your aunt and uncle's guest room/office, but hospitality and familial connections were of first priority back then.

This is where we get tripped up with the word *inn*. Traditional translations have obscured the meaning, but the Greek word *kataluma* refers more to a guest room than a hotel room. So rather than being turned

....
1   Luke 2:6 NASB.

away from hotels, Joseph found his relatives' house crammed with visiting family who were likely there for the census. The couple didn't come face-to-face with closed doors; they just had to make arrangements in the lower level of the house, which in an ancient setting was also a place that often housed livestock overnight to protect them from theft or harm. This lacks the theatrical cadence and tension of our modern way of summing up the story, but you can see that Mary and Joseph more likely delivered Jesus at an unplanned family reunion.

And yet the writer wants you to know there was no room for them in the usual place you would host pregnant family members. I mean, are you telling me that not one cousin, aunt, or uncle was willing to offer their (better) room to their family member's pregnant wife-to-be? That feels pretty indicting. Something was going on, and I believe "no guest room available for them" not only alludes to that but excavates something deeply personal in us as well.

We all come from families—and I say this knowing the word *family* has many different definitions. And no matter how wonderful that relational dynamic is, everyone butts up against the expectations that just naturally form in familial relationships from time to time. How you're supposed to act at the dinner table. What job you should have. How successful you should be. What kind of person you should marry. What beliefs you should have. What political party you should support. How you should wear your makeup. Whether or not you should get tattoos.

In the best light, these expectations occur because people love one another and want the best for the ones they care for. But we also know that we are love-insecure, and part of finding our love-security is checking off the list of what I'm doing right in order to have other people's approval. There is a pressure to conform to the group standard of what it looks like to represent this family name.

Maybe you've feared, just like I have, that your choices, identity, transformations would influence your family to put out the No Vacancy sign at the next gathering. Some of us have made choices in the pursuit of wholeness that there's no turning back from. Some of us have awakened to conclusions about our identity that make loved ones we've known our whole lives uncomfortable or silently distant. Some of us have transformed so much from what we once were that we don't even know how to talk the same way we did back then. It's a weird thing to be—to be a *be-ing*, I mean—and to discover, honor, and embody the reality of that be-ing-ness that we've been given to be.

It's interesting that the way Jesus came into the world didn't please everyone. He didn't come through the traditional way that appeased the family and cultural standards. While it's true that His incarnation was sung by a chorus of angelic hosts, His incarnation uncomfortably confronted many societal assumptions as well. And yet His incarnation was given a way, and beloved, your incarnation will be given a way too.

Your incarnation—the beginning of who you will become—may happen in the small town where no one expects anything like that to be birthed, but it will not go unnoticed by the heavenly hosts. In fact, they may even sing over it! A small group of people, possibly strangers, will witness it and dance a jig because of it. Some elders in your community may see your small incarnation and whisper prayers of thanksgiving for witnessing your humble revelation. And later on, in a way you least expected, international travelers may offer you precious gifts to carry you to the next phase of your life.

One of the ways we can experience God-with-Us presently is in the empathy that Jesus, Mary, and no-lines Joseph have for us as seen through our incarnation emerging in the midst of a family dynamic.

The story of Jesus' incarnation did not come without complications, but God provided room—a room—and the Giver of your incarnation will provide room for you too. It may not be the one you imagined. Or the one that pleases everyone. And it may leave you uninvited to your own family reunion. But it is the incarnation you have been given, and it comes with good news of great joy.

....

May you receive thanks for the gift of your incarnation.

The story of Jesus' incarnation did not come without **complications,** but **God** provided room—a room— and the Giver of your incarnation will provide **room for you too.**

CHAPTER 20

Go●p

"Today in the city of David there
has been born for you a Savior, who is
Christ the Lord."

LUKE 2:11 NASB

I've always loved Christmas. I love the lights. The eggnog. The music (nonstop until the 25th!). It's the holiday of holiday celebrations. But over the years, it has come to seem like the brand that we've created in celebration of Christmas feels void of any real hopeful significance.

The world has always been chaotic—full of wars, famines, loss, and hardship. But in our present reality, because of our global communication networks that bombard us with the details of every awful thing every single day, it feels super mega chaotic. The never-ending divisive and exhausting political battles. Images of innocent carnage from multiple mass shootings and acts of terrorism. The overwhelming clickbait stream of information that mostly tells us we're all doomed.

Then December hits, and the curated, clean aesthetics of safe shepherds, pleasant-smelling stables, picture-perfect stars, angels, wise men, and peppermint lattes just don't make sense in the face of this tsunami of darkness. This sanitized message of hope is as understandable as Charlie Brown's parents in this world on the brink of fearful despair.

Surprisingly, what *is* hopeful is the opposite of a polished and well-branded birth story. Where our hope *is* found is not in an ideal vision that is so far removed from our reality, but in the very messy and scandalous participation of human weakness. Everything about God Almighty incarnating through the vulnerable process of human birth confronts all of our ideas of overcoming power.

The sanitized brand we've created to celebrate Christmas aesthetically suggests we can only experience God-with-Us by cleaning up all of life's messy details. When everything is perfect, we'll get that Christmas tingle. But what we see through the details of the birthing process is that the Christ story is actually about a God who brings salvation into the world *through* all those messy details.

The labored breathing, groaning, shouting of a mother.
The powerlessness of a writhing, crying newborn.
The fear of not having a sanitized place to give birth.

What we see through the details of the **birthing process** is that the Christ story is actually about a God who brings **salvation** into the world *through* all those **messy details.**

Birthing in the ancient world was not like our reality. There was no ambulance or family car to drive you to the hospital to have a calculated and safe birth. Mary and Joseph didn't visit their favorite brunch spot before they checked in to have the King of Kings induced. They were forced by imperial decree to trek to a neighboring city where all of their familiarities were nonexistent. They were forced to deal with a situation that involved a lot of unknowns. They were forced to deal with the shocking biology of it all. The mucus plug. The amniotic fluid. The placenta. I've witnessed three births, and all of them brought me to tears. It's a beautiful experience . . . but not in any safe way.

Friends, so much comes out when a baby is born! Like

a clown car of human soup. Sometimes the mother poops while birthing. It's a detail mostly left out of baby birth books.

A *saving way* came into the world just like we did—in all of its goopy humanity. A birth is a rite of passage in human vulnerability, and the Almighty did not insulate Itself from participating in that. There is something overwhelmingly sacred about meditating on that reality during this time of year. That the Christ was born of blood—like we are. That the Christ partook in the powerless vulnerability of coming into the world naked and weak—like we often still feel. That the Christ was born into the fecal muck of human biology, which we seem to wade through for the rest of our lives.

Look, I'm not against Santa. Or presents. Or sanitized manger scenes. Or Best Buy gift cards. Keep all of it if you need to. But for me, the magic of Christmas is knowing that the saving Christ has always been in the fecal muck with us—and still is today. God-with-Us in all of our goopy humanity.

....

May the doorway to Advent wonder be opened by the shocking biology of it all.

CHAPTER 21

Breaking

"The virgin will conceive and
give birth to a son, and will call him
Immanuel."

ISAIAH 7:14

I remember when my daughter, Elsa (named before the Disney movie *Frozen*), came out of her mama.

I was standing next to my wife when it happened. Two years earlier, our first son, Anders, was born frank breech—meaning he was head up instead of head down, and one leg was doing a high kick while the other one pointed toward the exit. This in-utero Twister move made his birth a mandatory candidate for a C-section.

Elsa was healthy and head down, which made her a perfect candidate for a VBAC—vaginal birth after cesarean. (So many medical terms!) The labor was slow and long, and we visited the hospital a few times, only to be asked to go home and wait until my wife was fully dilated. When we were finally admitted for the birth, Holly had been in labor for a couple of days and was completely exhausted.

I remember being in the delivery room. I was holding

my wife's hand and her right leg while the doctor called out the play-by-play. The head crowned. It was time for the last push. "Puuuusssshhhh!" the doctor called out, and my wife breathed through the pain.

Elsa came out into the hands of the doctor, and we saw her for the first time. Then we looked at each other and instantly burst into tears. I remember the action being involuntary, as if I had witnessed something that could only be expressed in the breaking of my socially conformed demeanor. It was one of the most wonderful experiences I've had in my life.

To finally see what you have hoped for for so long is a breaking experience.

It's a healing breaking. Like cracking your back. Or hearing a sad song that breaks your heart in solidarity. Or witnessing a sappy commercial that somehow tickles your emotions and then you apologize to your friends on the couch for getting teary-eyed over it. We get emotional because we are witnessing something true. Not true as in an ideological list we use to draw lines and make teams. But something true that unites us. A moment of solidarity. A connective happening that awakens us to see that we are not alone. Like when a group of strangers is unanimously filled with joy as they watch fireworks together. Or when someone shares a tasty dish with someone else and says, "You *must* try this. It's so good!" Or when a newborn baby enters the room and everyone turns and looks because they know they are witnessing the magic of someone seen who just came from the unseen.

I wonder what broke in the room with Mary and Joseph? Probably tear ducts, because that happens to parents. But could it also have been the wall between ideology and incarnation? The culture they lived in was layered with centuries of prophecy and expectation regarding who the Messiah was supposed to be and what it was all supposed to look like. And yet here they were, being confronted with the real truth of that prophecy—that the hope of restoration had moved from words to presence. It wasn't just ideas. It was real. It must have been a healing breaking to hold that child and realize that the words of restoration paled in comparison to the physical presence of restoration.

Isn't that what we're hoping for this Advent? The breaking of the wall between ideology and incarnation? From words to real? Unfortunately, we don't get the newborn Christ child in the arms of Mary. But I offer you the image of it. Because that image points us to the universal truth of restoration: that the invitation is to move from words to presence.

Maybe it's our presence that needs to be broken open this Advent. Instead of adding more of our words to the centuries of expectations of what this is all supposed to do and be, maybe we need to reach out and hold what needs to be restored in our hands. Like people, or broken hearts, or systems, or perspectives, or beliefs, or policies, or our dashed hopes for a brighter tomorrow . . .

To finally see what you have hoped for for so long is a breaking experience. Our deepest hope is that God is truly with us in all this. That's what Christmas is meant to celebrate. But could it be that God has been with us in all this already?

God has just been waiting for us to move from words to presence so we can join God there.

....

May you believe in the gift of your presence. And may you bring that gift of presence to God's ongoing work of restoration.

CHAPTER 22

Unexpected

And there were shepherds living
out in the fields nearby, keeping watch
over their flocks at night.

LUKE 2:8

Divine revelation will come to you today through unexpected avenues you've probably ignored.

You may not know it, but a debate has been going on the last few years about how we're supposed to think about shepherds. The shepherd is an occupation found throughout the Bible. Many patriarchs of the Old Testament were shepherds at one time or another. The psalmist refers to the Lord as a shepherd.[1] Even the prophets refer to the coming Messiah as a shepherd. So being a shepherd is good, right?

But in Jesus' day, the shepherd had moved from hero to zero. If you were a shepherd, you were not the owner of the flock but the hired hand charged with taking care of the flock. Recent scholarship suggests that the opinion of shepherds in Jesus' day was that they were dishonest and thieving. Shepherding in a desert region

....

1 See Psalm 23.

required them to move around the land to find food and water, thus entailing their absence for long periods of time. Therefore, many claims were made against shepherds of pilfering other people's properties for resources, dealing in stolen sheep to grow flocks, and being religiously unclean for dealing with animals and breaking Sabbath law.

All that to say, shepherding was not the dream job of first-century Jewish children. In fact, most Jewish boys at that time began learning the Torah at a young age in the hope that they would become some kind of religious teacher when they got older. It was a hard road, and few made it. If you couldn't cut it in religious studies, you would learn a trade of a family member and do that for the rest of your life. Like a fisherman or a carpenter. Either it was your lot in life or you were unsuccessful at a lot of things in order to become a shepherd.

Yet it was shepherds to whom the angels were sent to announce the birth of Immanuel. Why? Because in true YHWH form, the Giver constantly uses the people we ignore to reveal the Giver's ways.

Sometimes it *is* through professional ministers, artists, authors, sages, monks, and gurus that we hear a divine invitation. If they're phonies, we'll know it, but mostly these women and men are fellow humans who have lived, learned, processed, and translated their experiences into a palpable wisdom that can be shared. We've heard their witness, and it rang true . . . so we buy their books, attend their conferences, and go to their concerts, hungry for the revelation they have to share. I'm not discrediting the avenues in which we *expect* to hear a divine revelation. Those individuals have done the secret personal work to bring forth a gift for the rest of us, and they deserve the attention they get.

But there's a deeper revelation that Jesus speaks to in all of the ignored and hidden aspects of the life we find ourselves in. Rest from anxiety is woven into the makeup of a lily. Providential supply is revealed in the eating habits of birds. And the Almighty Itself is waiting to be found hidden in someone described as the "least of these"—a neighborhood kid who spends too much time at your house or an unemployed dad waiting in a welfare line or maybe even the elderly Staples employee you mechanically interact with while replenishing your supply of ballpoint pens and computer paper.

See, God is bad at PR—on purpose—because the Divine has no interest in ending up on TV, being big on

Instagram, having Its own line of cookware at Target. That's too obvious. That's what we do with revelation. I understand that the honorable intent whenever we hear something life-changing is to want to share that with as many people as possible so they can hear it too. To get the most eyes on it, we make it big, loud, shiny, and shareable in hopes of going viral on social media and making a lot of lives better. But let's be honest. We also try to figure out if we can monetize it. We're always trying to make a profit off anything true, especially God.

Why God's revelations usually don't come through big flashy avenues is (1) God doesn't need any money via merchandise at retail stores, and (2) bigness doesn't ask the viewer/listener to have to transform to receive it . . . and God is all about the transformation.

The Giver of life hides revelation in the things we ignore because it is the work of humbling ourselves and asking to have eyes to see and ears to hear that truly transforms our hearts. It's in the unknowing of how things work—social norms, hierarchy of power, systemic injustice, gender inequality, race supremacy, physical and mental ableism, modes of intelligence, ageism—that we get a peek at love working its

The Giver of life hides revelation in the things we ignore because it is the work of humbling ourselves and asking to have eyes to see and ears to hear that truly transforms our hearts.

transforming will underneath the glitz and glamour of everything we produce.

A transformation was required for the townspeople to hear the proclamation of divine birth coming from the mouths of failed religion school shepherds. A transformation was required for the shepherds to believe they had been invited to be preachers of divine birth to their familiar neighbors. It was all very . . . unexpected.

So it is with you as well, that divine proclamation will come through very unexpected ways. It very well may be through the ignored and marginalized aspects of your life—the embarrassing, unsuccessful parts—that, if you take the time to listen, you'll begin to hear the angelic proclamation: "Do not be afraid. I bring you good news that will cause great joy for all the people. Today . . . a Savior has been born to you."[2]

. . . .

May you be given the eyes to see all the unexpected messengers carrying news of divine love birthing into today.

. . . .
2   Luke 2:10–11.

CHAPTER 23

Attention

"Where is the newborn king of the Jews? We saw his star as it rose, and we have come to worship him."

MATTHEW 2:2 NLT

Nothing can be truly known through observation. Only through participation.

This truth is perhaps best depicted in the film *Good Will Hunting*. There is a scene where Will, boy genius with a lot of relational trauma issues, played by actor Matt Damon, meets with his court-designated therapist Sean, played by Robin Williams. The day before, in Sean's office, Will, trying to escape the uncomfortableness of being asked vulnerable questions, pokes at Sean's character by critiquing a painting he did that hangs on the wall in his office, saying it's garbage, just like his career as a small-time community college psych professor and his recently ended marriage because of his wife's cancer. This gets under Sean's skin, and the meeting ends abruptly.

On a park bench the next day, Sean tells Will he stayed up all night long thinking about what Will had said about his painting, but he slept like a baby when he realized that Will was just a kid who has never left Boston. He knew Will could tell him all about Michelangelo from the books he'd read, but he couldn't tell Sean what it smells like in the Sistine Chapel, what it feels like to look up at that beautiful piece in Italy. Will could tell Sean all about marriage and probably recite some beautiful poetry about it, but he could never tell Sean what it feels like to wake up next to a person day after day for years and know you are truly loved. There's a difference between reading books about life and the actual risk and reward of living a life of travel, valor, love, and service. There is a deep knowing that can only be attained through participation.

The Bible tells us very little about the Magi. They are described as mysterious visitors from "the east" who have come to Jerusalem, looking for the child whose star they observed at its rising. They have an awkward run-in with King Herod, who knows nothing about this newborn king but now is secretly plotting this baby's destruction. They follow the star to Bethlehem, where upon seeing baby Jesus, they kneel down and worship Him, presenting Him with their three famous gifts of gold, frankincense, and myrrh. They return home, never to be heard of again, and their identity has remained a mystery to this day. Christians have been trying to figure out who they were for a very long time, as early as AD 200.

The running theory is that these Magi (more than three!) were a sort of upper-class, wealthy, star-watching celebrity priesthood most likely based in Persia. The Magi would have been familiar with the prophecies of a coming God-as-Man savior from the captivity of Israelite slaves several hundred years earlier in Babylon. So when they saw an unusual star in the west—maybe a supernova, a conjunction of planets, or just a good old-fashioned supernatural manifestation!—they made the long journey to find the king. Their identity will most likely always be shrouded in mystery, but at least we get (1) a catchy song out of it and (2) a fantastic model of what it means to pay attention.

They were paying attention. To what was around them, yes—the world, the sky, the stars. But they were also paying attention to how those exterior patterns were pointing to the interior patterns inside their hearts and souls. It may not be necessary to figure out the origins of the Magi, because the truth of their journey is what is truly transformational for us—that God places patterns inside us that will be revealed in the patterns of the exterior world.

The **truth** of the Magi's journey is what is truly **transformational** for us—that God places patterns **inside us** that will be revealed in the patterns of the exterior **world.**

Was the deep desire of the Magi to go on a road trip? I'm not saying the journey wasn't enjoyable, but remember, they didn't have AC and cruise control, just desert heat and camel humps. The deep desire of the Magi was to connect with the Creator of the world, and they trusted the Creator to reveal the interior journey of the soul in the exterior world around them. They wanted to know God, and they were willing to move from observation to participation in the pursuit of knowing. There was no promise that in traveling hundreds of miles in unknown territory they were going to find their way to this prophesied incarnation, but because of their deep desire to know God, they were willing to trust the signs in the sky to go and see.

Is it too fantastical to think that the Giver of your

spirit, who is also the Giver of this material world, will use both of those given realities to lead you to a deeper knowing? Are we not pointed to birds and flowers as signposts of God's benevolence? Are we not pointed to feeding the hungry and giving water to the thirsty as interactions with the King of Kings Himself?[1] Have you not witnessed something in the material world that made your soul whisper, "I think Someone's trying to get my attention"?

I remember early on in my art career sensing the invitation to go full-time. I had the traditional artist's part-time job as a waiter at a nearby restaurant, but I reached a point in my career where I was turning down art jobs because I couldn't get my shifts covered. I talked with other professional creatives and prayed for a time when I would know that the moment was right to put in my two weeks' notice at the restaurant.

I remember driving to work that day, and it seemed like all creation was affirming this decision. Tom Petty's "Time to Move On" played on the radio. Billboards for airlines and new condo construction screamed messages such as, "Ready for a Change?" and "Take the

---

1   See Matthew 6:25–34; 25:31–46.

Leap!" Even the migrating geese overhead proclaimed that this was a season of change and I was making the right decision. It was a leap of faith. I didn't know how it was going to turn out. But I could hear the Divine inviting me into this full-time identity, and I wanted to see if it was true. Others could do it. Why not me? I moved from observation to participation.

We may not be asked to travel hundreds of miles to experience the presence of a newborn king, but the stars leading you to a deeper knowledge of God may be just as mysterious now as they were back then. The wonder in God-with-Us is found in paying attention to the exterior patterns that illuminate the patterns within. If you are watching, you'll see them. Then you too will be asked to move from observation to participation in the ancient journey of knowing the Divine.

....

May you keep paying attention to what the outside illuminates inside.

CHAPTER 24

Need

The Child continued to grow and
become strong, increasing in wisdom;
and the grace of God was upon Him.

LUKE 2:40 NASB

It's easy to think of Jesus as not needing anyone.

Just out on a mission to save everyone. You know, clear
the temples, turn kingdoms upside down, take on the
religiously corrupt. Saviors don't need relationships!
Aren't saviors solo acts?

But Jesus called His disciples friends. He stayed at
friends' houses. He had a mom. And brothers and sisters.

He was fully human.

Have you, being fully human, ever lived a life separate
from relationships?

Did you not need someone to change your diapers as
a baby?

Did you not take a steady hand when learning how
to walk?

Did you not say, "Mama, look," when finishing your fourteenth Crayola masterpiece of the day?

Did you not confide a secret to your trusted bestie?

Did you not giggle until it hurt with someone at an inappropriate time?

Did you not let them buy you dinner when you were low on funds?

Did you not feel healed by a hug from someone who loved you?

Just like every human ever, at some moment Jesus sought a friend or a mom or a little sister for humor, compassion, nourishment, relatability, enjoyment. For belly laughs, hugs, inside jokes, maybe even high fives. That's the way being fully human works.

Did He not receive nourishment as a baby?

Did He not live in a house that His parents provided?

Did He not wear clothes that others had meticulously woven?

It's easy to think of us as needing Jesus, but it's pretty scandalous to think that Jesus would need us . . .

Did He not learn to read from attentive teachers?

Did He not learn a trade so He could make a living?

Did He not join His voice to the chorus of singing?

Did He not know the joy of having friends?

Jesus' incarnation is participating in the same
dynamics we all participate in . . .

Which is no one who is fully human is an island.

And we need each other to be fully human.

It's easy to think of us as needing Jesus, but it's pretty
scandalous to think that Jesus would need us . . .

Why is that again?

. . . .

May you receive the gift of reciprocal love.

CHAPTER 25

Fear

"Be not afraid; for behold, I bring
you good tidings of great joy which
shall be to all the people."

LUKE 2:10 ASV

"Be Not Afraid" could be a legitimate substitution for "Merry Christmas."

This command kicked off the first message spoken after four hundred years of divine silence. It was directed to Zechariah as he learned of the upcoming birth of his son, John the Baptist. It was said to Mary as she received the message that she would be bearing the Savior through her virgin womb. It was spoken to Joseph as he pondered quietly divorcing his betrothed for her seemingly adulterous pregnancy. It was sung to the shepherds as they were hired to be the first incarnation preachers in the coming kingdom. And it is announced to you today as you celebrate this historical moment that is still happening in your midst.

Why it was a shock to see angels is left to our imaginations. I'm guessing most of our assumptions about that experience involve a robust sound and light show. We imagine blinding light, the haloic glow of a nongender

humanoid form in a white robe (or loose pantsuit)
delivering a divine speech backgrounded by the sonic
persuasions of heavenly chords.

But what gave us this vision? Scripture? Nope. Mostly
television and movie scenes. It's not that it didn't happen
that way, but it wasn't necessarily such a big production.
The account of the shepherds just says, "The glory of
the Lord shone around them,"[1] implying that there was
light—possibly because it was nighttime and it would've
been hard to see some messengers in the dark. In all
the other cases, it could have been very simple and less
glittery than we imagine. Just a glorious stranger delivering an unbelievable message in a familiar setting. I think
the invitation of the glory of the Lord that shines is less
in the light show and more in the message.

"The glory of the Lord" has many etymological roots,
but they all point to an idea of heaviness or weight
alongside the notion of respect and honor. If you can
imagine swimming in an open body of water, and all
of a sudden, a fifty-foot humpback whale is swimming slowly by you, singing its baleen soliloquy, after
you pee in the sea, you are overwhelmed by the glory

....
1 Luke 2:9.

of that whale—the enormity of size, presence, and force in that moment. Your fragility in the presence of its immensity demands your respect. The writers of the Bible describe this same kind of experience, but without the size parameters of oceanic mammals. They allude to immense weightiness in an interaction that demands their respect.

Maybe the weightiness is simply the awakening that God is real. That the hidden, much larger spiritual realm is really there, and that the way you have been assessing everything has fallen apart. And you're left in the weighty space of not knowing what to think anymore. A message from the Divine must start with "Be not afraid" because it is shattering the security you've found in limited conclusions:

Existence is a curse to endure.

A message from the

"Be not afraid" because it

you've found in

Our bodies are just flawed meatsuits full of
disappointment.

Divine encounters only happen with worthy saints
on mountaintops or in sacred places.

The Almighty can't wait to be wrathful toward all
the sinful malarkey taking place on this earth.

We deserve to be left out because of our glaring
inability to be faithful.

And yet the messengers who "stand in the presence of
God"[2] are astonished by our limited conclusions, for
their message is a proclamation of good news:

that existence, in all its seeming absurdity, is not
a curse to endure but the very gift that the

....
2   Luke 1:19.

Divine must start with
is **shattering** the security
limited **conclusions.**

Giver of existence wants you to receive and
participate in

that it's good to be in your body, for all kinds of
miracles happen through it

that divine encounters happen in the humblest of
places, like at your job, in your kitchen, in the
headspace of making hard decisions

that the Almighty didn't enter the world as a
judgmental titan set on condemning it but
as a loving participant whose ultimate work
of healing came through His ultimate loving
participation

that Love is intentionally inclusive in Its restoration
invitation of all things and isn't worried about
not accomplishing what It has set out to do

Don't get me wrong. I'm down with an angelic visit.
I'd love to see firsthand what Luke means when he
writes, "The glory of the Lord shone around them"—
and I'd for sure make a painting of it. Think about how
famous that painting would be if I could depict it! Not
in a celebrity way, but in a true way. Like an image
that helps the world find a firm place to stand in the
quicksand of insecurity.

I haven't had an angelic visit like that, but I give you this image of a little baby being born into our world—one like so many others before me have depicted—because maybe the glory of the Lord shining around is already happening to me, to you, to us when we consider the weight of that incarnation in our lives today.

Maybe the place we experience God-with-Us today is in the very fears we have about our own lives, our own world, our own future. The fears that keep us from believing that anything can be different. The fears that make the silence of the Divine feel like centuries have passed. The fears that we are here all on our own. The fears we will be holding at our upcoming angelic visit.

Today, let our fears be the starting place of divine connection, because if a messenger from heaven were to show up with an announcement of good tidings of great joy, a message that will change everything, historically that proclamation would begin with the greeting "Be Not Afraid"—or, the way we say it today, "Merry Christmas."

....

May you be not afraid, for Love has drawn near.

Afterword

"Jesus Christ is Lord"[1]—and that's nothing I believe I have to convince you of.

For one thing, most of us are non-convincible. Substantial evidence shows that human beings ignore facts that contradict what they want to believe. See any political debate in your Facebook feed. For another, people who want to convince you of anything are annoying. See some religious people . . .

Unless . . . *unless* . . . you're grateful they introduced you to something you end up loving. Like a mind-blowing sushi spot. Or a new favorite song. Or a book. Or a friend. Or a story. Or a way of seeing everything that renews in you a desire to say yes to the life you find yourself in, no matter how complicated it is.

....
1   Philippians 2:11.

We honor each other with titles like "survivor of," "veteran of," "defeater of" when we witness the ways people have wholeheartedly participated in the lives they would not have chosen for themselves. It's especially difficult in times of war, cancer, depression, divorce, death of a loved one, death of a dream . . . because the temptation is to ignore the pain of reality instead of going through it. We give honoring titles to those who have gone through the pain of reality, because we also can attest to how hard it is to just go through reality.

This reality. You know, the one you and I find ourselves in. The one Jesus found Himself in too. The one we still find Him participating in. Which brings us back to the original question of whether Christmas is a memorial service or a birthday party. Is it something that happened long ago, or is it something that's happening right now?

Not long after the first Christmas, the apostle Paul wrote a letter to a group of Jesus believers in Philippi, encouraging them in difficult times. In a rather poignant moment, he invited them to refrain from selfish ambition and vain conceit. To be humble and to value others above themselves. He said they shouldn't look to their own interests, but to the

interests of others.[2] By doing this, they would participate in the same outlook on life that Jesus had:

> Who, being in very nature God,
>> did not consider equality with God something
>>> to be used to his own advantage;
> rather, he made himself nothing
>> by taking the very nature of a servant,
>> being made in human likeness.
> And being found in appearance as a man,
>> he humbled himself
>> by becoming obedient to death—
>>> even death on a cross!
> Therefore God exalted him to the highest place
>> and gave him the name that is above every name,
> that at the name of Jesus every knee should bow,
>> in heaven and on earth and under the earth,
> and every tongue acknowledge that Jesus Christ is
>> Lord,
>> to the glory of God the Father.[3]

Isn't it a bit audacious to claim that everyone everywhere will come to the same conclusion on a specific
topic? That seems ludicrous in our current world. I

....

2   See Philippians 2:3–4.
3   Philippians 2:6–11.

mean, I just wrote a book about Jesus, but I still don't like someone telling me what conclusion I'm going to come to. Don't take away my agency, Paul! But Paul, quoting Isaiah,[4] doesn't seem worried about making this claim because it's less about making a convincing argument and more about witnessing an honest life.

We can see this honest life when we contemplate the sacred texts written by those who witnessed divine participation in the midst of their everyday lives. Granted, Jesus had some extracurricular activities during His own incarnation, but He did not bypass the hardships of being human. He participated from womb to tomb, and everything in between. It is this honest life offered for the healing of the world that gives Him the title of Lord, or the One Who Has Authority Over. Not as a tyrannical know-it-all, but as a full participant who now holds the keys of life and death and offers a way to unlock it all.

At least that's the invitation in our lives today: to witness that same arrival of God-with-Us in all the expected and unexpected realities of our human lives. An honest Advent that leads to an honest hope, which perhaps saves us from two unholy polarities—the empty

....
4   See Isaiah 45:23.

That's the **invitation** in our lives today: to witness that same arrival of **God-with-Us** in all the expected and unexpected realities of our human lives. An honest Advent that leads to an **honest hope.**

positivity and blind optimism that masquerade as hope (yet are never honest about the realities of pain and death), or the surrender to despair and hopelessness. Honest hope is birthed in the realness in between the messy headlines of today's news. It invites us to consider every situation, no matter how despairing, as something we don't have to walk through alone, but as the very birthplace for divine participation.

But like I said, it's nothing I believe I can convince you of. As it was for Mary and Joseph, the Magi, the shepherds, and the saints throughout the ages, myself included, it's just an invitation to you to come and see for yourself.

Thanks

I want to thank . . .

Holly, my wife—for being my biggest fan and never letting me quit. You basically did everything so I had the time to write this book. I love you so much. Thanks for loving me so well.

Anders, Elsa, and Jones—for being the way to a deeper life.

Erick and Merrily—for just about everything.

Joy Eggerichs Reed—for being my fantastic agent and a literal unicorn.

Justin McRoberts—for teaching me so much about being an author and a genuine human being.

My editor, Stephanie Smith—for pursuing me and pushing me to be a better author.

Mica May—for letting me use her office while I wrote this book.

Kurt Kroon—for tossing the theological ball with me.

Morris Dirks—for giving me a place to be poor in spirit.

I also want to thank Bellingham Lifers, Houston Hamptons, Vancouver Nitehawks, ATL Richs, McGraw Tribe, Aurora Karaoke Crew, Lucky House Guys Night, South Everett Wannabes, Portland Eccentrics, Raleigh Ragamuffins, Mukilteo OGs, and all the other magical places in the world where I have fantastic friends. You're my favorite part of being alive. Thank you, Cascade Church, Union Chapel, Church on Morgan, Ecclesia Houston, and Imago Dei Community, for inviting me to be just as I am in your community.

The gift of incarnation can only be received through participation. Thank You, Giver, for this gift.

About the Author

SCOTT ERICKSON is a touring painter, performance artist, and creative curate who mixes autobiography, aesthetics, and comedic narrative to create experiences that speak to our deepest stories.

He's currently touring a one-man show, *Say Yes: A Liturgy of Not Giving Up on Yourself*, where he walks us through the very personal and universal conversation about the death of a dream and the overwhelming voice of Giving Up in our lives.

He is the coauthor of *Prayer: Forty Days of Practice* and *May It Be So*, a spiritual director to brave women and men, and a professional dishwasher for his food-blogging wife.

Scott lives in Austin, Texas, with his wife and three children.

www.scottericksonart.com
Instagram: @scottthepainter